Protectionism: Threat to International Order

Order
The impact on Developing Countries

Commonwealth Secretariat,
Marlborough House, London SW1

Published by
The Commonwealth Secretariat

May be purchased from
Commonwealth Secretariat Publications
Marlborough House
London SW1Y 5HX

ISBN 0 85092 219 4

Price £2.00

Foreword by Commonwealth Secretary-General

When they met in Melbourne in October 1981 Commonwealth Heads of Government had much to say on the subject of trade and protectionism. They expressed anxiety over the trend to increased protectionism, awareness of the importance of expansion of world trade to economic recovery and growth, and agreement that governments should make further efforts to reduce tariff and non-tariff barriers and achieve international accord on effective rules covering resort to emergency safeguards. They took special note that little progress had been made in eliminating quantitative restrictions against certain categories of manufactured exports of particular importance to developing countries, that the process of reducing barriers to trade in agricultural products had scarcely begun, and that the export of processed commodities continued to be constrained by trade barriers which escalate with the degree of processing.

It was against this backdrop that they welcomed the proposal for a Ministerial Meeting of the GATT in 1982. But they did not stop there. Given their strong interest in the issues involved and with a view to assisting their deliberations, they requested me to bring together a group of independent, high-level, Commonwealth experts to investigate the impact of protection on developing countries' trade. The Report that follows is the work of that Commonwealth Expert Group. As is customary, members of the Group served in their personal capacities and not as representatives of institutions, governments or countries. Their views, therefore, do not necessarily represent those of Commonwealth governments, individually or collectively.

Since Melbourne, there has been a further deterioration in the world economic situation. Reduced demand combined with protectionism has greatly curtailed exports from developing countries. Their imports have in turn been lowered and, with further adverse effects from tighter borrowing conditions in capital markets, imports by developing countries are becoming less significant as a factor in sustaining economic activity in the North. Partly as a result of these developments the expansion of world trade, which has slowed down considerably in recent years, has now come to a halt. Unless special efforts are made, external trade is now not in a position to play its customary role as an engine of growth. With domestic demand depressed in many developed countries, recovery remains uncertain. It is against this sombre background that the Commonwealth Expert Group has produced its Report. As the Expert Group puts it, there is a danger "that the present international depression may become still deeper and more protracted".

The Expert Group considers today's trade problems and the rise of protectionism as having deeper and more long-term origins than the current recession. Trade policy has not only not kept pace with new demands, but is even retrogressing in traditional areas. Malfunctioning has become pervasive, and protectionism, implemented in its most damaging forms, poses a threat to international order. The Expert Group appropriately, therefore, has addressed short and long-term issues and their Report calls for a phased approach to major changes to develop a more relevant trading regime. The Group has pointed the way ahead; it is a way which provides scope for Commonwealth leadership in an area where there is strong mutuality of interest between North and South. The Report provides an opportunity which must not be allowed to pass.

In presenting its Report, the Expert Group expressed the hope that it would be useful to Commonwealth governments in preparing for the GATT Ministerial Meeting in November and to the wider international community when discussing trade issues in the GATT, UNCTAD and other bodies in the period ahead. I share this hope, and have pleasure in presenting to Commonwealth governments and to the wider international community the unanimous conclusions of an independent group of Commonwealth experts on a subject of great global significance.

Shridath S Ramphal

Letter of Presentation

Marlborough House,
London, SW1.

2 July 1982

H.E. Mr. S.S. Ramphal,
Commonwealth Secretary-General,
Marlborough House,
Pall Mall,
London, SW1.

Dear Secretary-General,

We are grateful for your trust and confidence in appointing us to serve as the Commonwealth Expert Group on the impact of protection on the trade of the developing countries, which you were requested to set up by Commonwealth Heads of Government at their Meeting in Melbourne in September/October 1981.

We transmit herewith our Report which represents the unanimous conclusions of the Group. We trust that it will be useful to Commonwealth governments in their preparations for the GATT Ministerial Meeting to which it is immediately directed. We hope that it will also be of advantage to the wider international community in their discussions and negotiations on the issues in the GATT, UNCTAD and other bodies in the period ahead.

In accordance with the terms of our appointment, we sign the Report in our personal capacities, and not as representatives of governments, institutions or countries. We should like to express our thanks for the support and encouragement you provided and the great interest you showed in our work. We should like also to express our appreciation of the unfailing assistance we have enjoyed from the Secretariat.

Please accept, Secretary-General, the expression of our highest consideration.

Alec Cairncross

Mohamed Ariff

G.K. Helleiner

Satya Nandan

Philip Ndegwa

E.M. Ojala

F.B. Rampersad

E. Olu Sanu

Manmohan Singh

R.H. Snape

Augustine H.H. Tan

vi

Contents

Preface

1.   At their Melbourne meeting in October 1981, Commonwealth Heads of Government requested the Secretary-General to commission a group of independent high-level experts:

"to investigate the impact of protection on developing country trade and report in time to assist governments in their preparations for the proposed GATT Ministerial Meeting. They agreed the group would examine the effects of protection on developing countries, including the impact of tariff and non-tariff barriers on industrial and agricultural products. In this respect the group should consider, inter alia, the question of emergency safeguards, and non-conventional measures which, among other things, include such matters as voluntary export restraints and orderly marketing arrangements; structural adjustment; the escalation of tariffs and trade barriers that constrain the expansion of trade in processed commodities; and the adequacy of existing arrangements for the settlement of disputes".[1]

2.   The list of members of the Group is at Appendix 4.

3.   The Group held three meetings in London in February, April and June/July 1982 and submitted its Report to the Commonwealth Secretary-General on 2 July 1982.

4.   The immediate purposes of this Report are to contribute to the deliberations of the ministerial meeting of the GATT Contracting Parties which is to be held in November 1982 and to assist governments in their preparations for that meeting. In preparing their Report, the Group was aware of the relevance of their Terms of Reference to other negotiations such as those in UNCTAD VI and the prospective Global Round of Negotiations, at both of which discussions on protectionism will no doubt feature strongly. The Report may also be timely in making available to the

1

public an up-to-date assessment of the more tangible effects of protection in its different forms on the trade of the developing countries.

5.   We review in Chapter 1 the recent economic developments that form the background to the rising tide of protectionism and draw attention to the dangers confronting the developing countries. Chapter 2 deals with the new forms of protection and the disorder they introduce into the world's trading system, while Chapter 3 examines the extent and form of protection against different groups of products of particular interest to developing countries. In Chapters 4 and 5 we go on to analyse the cost of protection to developing and developed countries and the ways in which the objectives of the second group could be pursued with least harm to the first. In Chapter 6 we discuss the various preferential arrangements that have been introduced in favour of developing countries and other trade measures of which they have taken advantage. In Chapter 7 we consider the weaknesses of the existing international machinery for regulating the trading system, including the GATT, and discuss how it might be improved and how an orderly trading system might be re-built. A brief summary of our main conclusions and recommendations is presented in Chapter 8.

6.   The Group wishes to acknowledge the invaluable advice and assistance it received from a number of persons during the course of its work. Among these are Ambassadors Donald McPhail of Canada and Anthony Hill of Jamaica, Chairman and a Vice-Chairman respectively of the GATT Contracting Parties; Messrs. Reinaldo Figueredo, Colin Greenhill and Gary Sampson of the UNCTAD Secretariat; Messrs. Jan Tumlir and Nicolas Marian of the GATT Secretariat; Dr. Vincent Cable of the Overseas Development Institute; Mr. Rodney de C. Grey, Special Adviser, Government of Ontario; and Messrs. Carl Wright and Allan Cave of the Commonwealth Trade Union Council.

1. Commonwealth Heads of Government: The Melbourne Communiqué, paragraph 59 (Commonwealth Secretariat, London, 1981).

1. The Background to Protectionism

"The first business of all trading nations must be to try to keep international trade continually expanding, for unless it is expanding, the changes in the relative importance of countries which circumstances continually demand cannot be achieved without friction. The world must continue to make the problems of each the official concern of all, so that they may be solved by discussion and mutual concession".

Arthur Lewis, 1949

The problems of commercial policy which we have been asked to consider cannot be isolated from the wider issues confronting the world economy in the 1980s. We begin, therefore, by analysing the more important trends at work in international trade and finance, the prospects for the 1980s and the problems posed by the changes in progress.

An Unstable World Economy

1.2   The past decade has been marked by great turbulence in the world economy. This took a number of forms of which the most persistent was price inflation. In all the industrial countries in the OECD except Switzerland, consumer prices have risen since 1970 by at least 80 per cent and in some the rise has been more than fourfold. Inflation has continued through boom and slump, the rise in retail prices averaging over 10 per cent in the industrial countries, even in years of depressed activity like 1980 and 1981. In the developing countries inflation has reached still higher rates, averaging about 40 per cent in 1980 and again in 1981.

1.3   In the developed countries inflation went with slower growth and rising unemployment: not only inadequate levels and slower growth in output associated with failure to maintain full employment but slower growth in productivity as well. In the later seventies economic growth was at a rate averaging about half that experienced in the 1950s and 1960s. It

3

has been lower still in 1980 and 1981 — just over 1 per cent. This slowing down was particularly marked in manufacturing and was reflected in rising unemployment on a scale unknown since the early 1930s. The reduction in employment in turn tended to be heaviest in manufacturing, the sector most affected by international trade.

1.4 Instability in prices, output and employment was associated on the one hand with monetary expansion and currency instability and on the other with successive jolts from large and abrupt increases in the world price of oil to which importing countries had difficulty in adjusting. Both of these factors made for severe international imbalance, with abnormally large surpluses and deficits in balances of payments, wide fluctuations in exchange rates, large-scale movements of volatile funds from one country to another and a rapidly growing burden of international indebtedness concentrated on the developing countries.

1.5 This external instability reacted back on domestic economies. Deficit countries felt compelled to reduce their deficits even at the cost of restricting economic activity; efforts to prevent a slide in exchange rates led to reliance on higher interest rates when these were already moving up as expectations of continuing inflation became firmer; and these higher interest rates presented increasingly difficult problems for the countries that were borrowing abroad to finance their deficits. For many of the developing countries in particular, higher interest rates, together with increased dependence on borrowing from private banks and a consequent shortening of maturities, all at a time of reduced export growth, created serious debt-servicing problems. High interest rates also contributed to downward pressures on primary commodity prices through their effects upon private stockholding decisions, intensifying balance of payments pressures on countries with limited access to commercial borrowing.

1.6 Instability in its various forms, and the uncertainty to which it gave rise, narrowed the options open to governments and disposed them to take resolute action against what they saw as its prime source: inflation. In the struggle, economic activity inevitably suffered so that by 1982 there was a wide gap between the level of demand and output in the industrial countries and their full economic potential. Unemployment developed on such a vast scale that the resumption of expansionary policies, even if successful, would take many years to reduce the amount of slack to the levels experienced in the 1960s and 1970s. The process of recovery is likely to be slowed down by the fears of governments that it might bring back inflation and by the danger from which these fears derive, that too rapid an expansion would encounter supply bottlenecks as demand took new directions and met with inadequate capacity.

4

1.7   It is not easy to assess the prospects for the rest of this decade. There is a danger that the present international depression may become still deeper and more protracted. On the other hand, once recovery begins and the slack in the industrial economies is gradually absorbed, this may permit a temporary acceleration in economic growth as output rises to rejoin the previous trend. It would seem prudent to allow for an intermediate prospect in which the world economy remains plagued by instability, running well below capacity, and registering rates of expansion lower than in the days of the post-war secular boom.

The Slowdown in Market Expansion

1.8   Slower growth in the industrial economies has had its inevitable effect on international trade. After 1973, world markets became less buoyant and the volume of trade expanded at less than half the rate of the previous decade (see Table 1.1).

1.9   Measured in current prices, the growth of world trade shown in Table 1.1 looks impressive. But the fast rates of expansion under each heading correspond more to the inflationary movement of prices than to the comparatively slow growth in volume. This is particularly true of fuels, where the whole of the increase by value since 1973 is accounted for by price rises. On the other hand, agricultural produce, where the rate of increase by volume was well maintained, experienced a relative price decline and was the slowest growing of the four groups in value terms. By 1980 the share of agricultural exports in the value of world trade had fallen to a post-war low of 15 per cent while fuels had expanded to nearly a quarter.

1.10   Measured in constant prices, the change in trend was greatest in fuels where there was a net contraction in the volume of trade between 1973 and 1980 and a further contraction thereafter. By contrast, trade in agricultural products, for rather special reasons, seems to have maintained a comparatively steady rate of expansion. Manufactures, much the largest element in the total, slowed down from a rate of growth of 11 per cent per annum to an average of 5 per cent in the later 1970s and 3½ per cent over the last two years.

1.11   In those two years world trade has virtually ceased to expand. In 1980 it rose in volume by 1 per cent and in 1981 it stagnated. While trade in agricultural products and in manufactures continues to grow, the increase under these headings was more or less offset by the fall in petroleum exports by 10 per cent in 1980 and a further 14 per cent in 1981. The persistence of expansion in trade in manufactures, in spite of the sluggishness of world demand and the protectionist pressures which we discuss in this Report, is mainly to be attributed to the continued growth in

5

import demand in developing countries. Three-quarters of the increase in volume of world trade in manufactures in 1981 was due to the expansion in exports to developing countries: 45 per cent to members of OPEC and 30 per cent to the others.[1]

TABLE 1.1
Growth in International Trade, 1963-81

| | Value of world trade billion dollars | | Average annual percentage increase in world trade | | | |
| | | | by value | by volume | | |
	1973	1980	1973-80	1963-73	1973-80	1979-81
Manufactures	348	1,089	18	11	5	3½
Minerals (excl. fuels)	32	91	16 }	7	4 }	-9
Fuels	63	468	33 ⌡		-4 ⌡	
Agricultural products	121	296	14	4	4½	3
Total	574	1,973	19	8½	4	¾

Sources: GATT, *International Trade 1980/81; International Trade in 1981 and Present Prospects,* Press Release 1313, 23 March 1982.

1.12   The slowdown in market expansion has been coupled with the introduction of fresh barriers to trade that bear particularly heavily on the developing countries. In reviewing these barriers we have thought it natural to examine them from the point of view of the developing countries as a group as well as from the point of view of the industrial countries that impose them. We have not, however, lost sight of the wide differences between the countries included in each group and the consequent differences in the impact of the new protectionism on individual developing countries, as well as the differences in the forms and extent of protectionism in individual developed countries. For many primary producing countries, the old agricultural protectionism is at least as damaging as the new industrial protectionism and has indeed taken new and more damaging forms. In the case of manufactures, what has been achieved so painfully in lower tariffs has for many developing countries been altogether offset, and more than offset, by quantitative and other limitations that are most severe where the developing countries have proved most successful.

1.13   Trade does, however, provide a bond between the developing and developed countries. In spite of all barriers, the trade has continued to grow. It is in the interests of both groups of countries to encourage this growth: for the developed countries it brings a welcome expansion in export markets when production is flagging and for the developing countries it is an indispensable element in their development.

The Impact of Recent Trends on the Developing Countries

1.14 Many of the developing countries continued to make progress in the 1970s at a rate that compared favourably with the record of earlier years. While the industrial countries suffered a severe setback, with rates of growth in GDP substantially lower after 1973 than in the previous quarter of a century, the developing countries as a group, including the oil exporters, maintained on the average, rates close to those experienced in the 1960s. On one reckoning the growth in per capita real income for the entire group (including the oil producers and taking account of the favourable change in the terms of trade that this involves) was appreciably higher.[2] This outcome, however, largely reflects the rise in oil prices, the major oil-exporting countries enjoying an average improvement in per capita real income of over 11 per cent per annum in the 1970s compared with one of under 1 per cent in the previous decade. Per capita real income in the oil-importing developing countries did not grow faster but rather more slowly in the 1970s. Moreover there were wide differences between the different groups making up the total. While the fast-growing exporters of manufactures experienced an acceleration in the growth of per capita income between the 1960s and 1970s from 3.5 per cent to 4.0 per cent, the least developed countries, where real income per capita had shown no increase in the 1960s, registered negative growth in the 1970s. In about half the developing countries for which there are figures, per capita growth was less than 2 per cent per annum in the 1970s while in the previous decade the corresponding proportion was only one-third.[3] Whatever the record for the decade as a whole, more recent experience is disturbing. By 1981 average per capita incomes in the developing countries as a group had ceased to increase.

1.15 In the 1970s the trade of the developing countries showed the same range of experience as their per capita growth. Between 1973 and 1980 the OPEC countries increased their exports from $42 billion to $297 billion and their share of world trade from 7.3 per cent to 15.6 per cent, thanks entirely to the rise in oil prices.[4] The non-oil developing countries as a group increased their exports from $68 billion to $245 billion and slightly improved their share but at a slower rate than in the preceding decade. Within the group some enjoyed a rapid growth in export volume while others suffered a contraction. For the fast-growing exporters of manufactures, for example, the rate of expansion in exports averaged 11.8 per cent in the 1970s, compared with 5.8 per cent in the 1960s while for the least

7

developed countries, whose exports had grown by 4.4 per cent per annum in the 1960s, there was an actual fall over the 1970s (see Table 1.2). Since the terms of trade were decidedly less favourable to the oil-importers at the end of the decade than at the beginning, the movement in purchasing power over imports was less favourable, both to the fast-growing exporters of manufactures and to the least developed countries, than the change in their exports might suggest.[5]

TABLE 1.2
Growth in Volume of Exports from Developing
Countries and Purchasing Power of their
Exports, 1960-80

	Growth in export volume (per cent per annum)		Growth in purchasing power of exports (per cent per annum)	
	1960-70	1970-80	1960-70	1970-80
Major oil exporters	8.6	–1.4	7.2	17.9
Non-oil exporting developing countries	5.1	7.6	5.7	4.5
Of which:				
Fast-growing exporters of manufactures	5.8	11.8	7.0	8.2
Least developed countries	4.4	–0.4	3.6	–2.2
All developing countries	6.4	3.1	6.2	10.0

For country groupings, see Appendix 3.
Source: UNCTAD, *Trade and Development Report, 1981*, p.38.

1.16 Over the past two years the earlier buoyancy of exports from the non-oil developing countries has largely disappeared. As Table 1.3 brings out, the volume of exports for each of the main groups of developing countries grew at a progressively slower rate and the terms of trade either became steadily less favourable or (in the special case of the net oil exporters) ceased to improve. For the entire group, purchasing power over exports, which was increasing rapidly between 1976 and 1979, grew in 1980 and 1981 by not much over 1 per cent per annum.[6]

TABLE 1.3
Trade of Non-Oil Developing Countries, 1968-81

	Volume of exports				Growth in purchasing power of exports[1]			
	Percentage changes from preceding year							
	Annual 1968-72	1979	1980	1981	Annual 1968-72	1979	1980	1981
All non-oil developing countries	8.4	9.4	5.6	3.9	8.4	9.1	1.1	1.6
Of which:								
Net oil exporters	5.3	9.1	6.0	3.3	3.8	26.2	13.7	2.9
Net oil importers	9.3	8.7	5.0	3.2	8.9	5.2	–2.2	0.1
Of which:								
Major exporters of manufactures	11.8	10.4	5.6	4.4	12.6	7.0	2.6	3.4
Low income countries	5.5	3.9	1.5	–1.5	6.1	–3.8	–13.8	–9.7
Other net oil importers	6.7	7.2	5.0	2.1	5.2	5.1	–7.3	–3.9

1. Export earnings deflated by import prices.

For country groupings, see Appendix 3.

Source: IMF, *World Economic Outlook*, Appendix B, Table 13, April 1982.

Changes in Developing Countries' Trade

1.17 The experience of the OPEC countries as a group has been fundamentally different from that of the rest of the developing world. Not only did their level of real income and the value of their exports grow much faster after 1973 but they were also for much of the time in very large surplus on current account and free, almost without exception, from balance of payments constraints. They were in addition a rapidly expanding market, and one where other developing countries took an increasing share. Thus few of them were plagued by the trade and financial difficulties besetting other countries. Most had not the least difficulty in finding a market for their exports (at least until very recently), whatever the

9

impediments some countries continued to put in the way of fuel imports. They enjoyed an almost continuous surplus on trade account. And so, far from struggling with increasing debt obligations at rising rates of interest, they were ranked with the creditors and able to draw an expanding income from external assets.

1.18 We can therefore for present purposes set the OPEC group of countries on one side and concentrate on the other developing countries. As we have seen, these have taken a slowly growing share of world trade. They have also taken a growing share of imports into the OPEC countries and their trade both with OPEC and, to a lesser extent, with one another has expanded as a proportion of their total trade (see Table 1.4). Over 60 per cent of their trade, however, is still with the industrial countries. That is where their main markets lie and it is this trade that is the usual source of the issues of commercial policy with which we are concerned.

TABLE 1.4
Exports from Developing Countries (excluding OPEC), 1973-80

Exports to:	Value of exports ($ billion)			
	1973		1980	
Industrial countries	47.7	(70%)	153.0	(62%)
OPEC countries	2.4	(4%)	17.5	(7%)
Other developing countries	12.5	(19%)	54.0	(22%)
Total[1]	68.3	(100%)	245.0	(100%)

1. Including Australia, New Zealand, South Africa and centrally planned economies. For country groupings, see Appendix 3.

Source: GATT, *International Trade 1980/81*, Table A22.

1.19 In spite of the difficulties restricting this trade, it continued to grow throughout the 1970s. In value terms, as Table 1.5 shows, the increase in exports to the industrial countries was more than threefold; in volume terms it was probably only about 20 per cent. Of the three principal elements in the total, fuel fell in volume but more than doubled its share of export earnings; other primary produce (including agriculture) rose comparatively little in volume and shrank from 58 to 39 per cent of total exports by value; manufactures were the one element to grow strongly in volume and formed an increasing proportion of total exports.

10

TABLE 1.5
Exports from Developing Countries to
Industrial Countries, 1973-80

	1973 at current prices ($ bn)		1980 at current prices ($ bn)		1980 at 1973 prices ($ bn)	1973-80 Increase in volume %
Exports from non-OPEC countries						
Fuels	4.3	(9%)	37.0	(24%)	3.7	−14
Other primary products	27.8	(58%)	59.5	(39%)	29.75	+ 7
Manufactures	15.1	(32%)	56.5	(37%)	25.45	+ 68.5
Total (incl. other)	47.7	(100%)	153.0	(100%)	58.9	+ 23.5
Exports from OPEC countries	32.6		220.0		25.5	−22
Exports from all developing countries	80.3		373.0		84.4	+ 5

Source: GATT, *International Trade 1980/81*, Table A22.

1.20 Primary produce (excluding fuels) is now almost equalled in importance by manufactures, while fuels — even with the omission of OPEC countries — are nearly two-thirds as large an earner of foreign exchange as all other primary produce put together. This picture is radically different from the situation twenty or more years ago. It has been estimated, for example, that in 1958 manufactures formed only about 5 per cent of the exports of non-industrial countries to industrial countries, compared with 71 per cent for primary produce other than fuels, and 23 per cent for fuels (a proportion inflated by inclusion of OPEC countries).[7]

1.21 What emerges clearly from this comparison is the overwhelming effect on international trade of higher oil prices and the remarkable growth

11

of manufactured exports from the developing countries, especially in comparison with the slow growth in exports of primary produce. Only a limited group of oil-producing countries profited directly from the rise in oil prices although a number of other developing countries profited indirectly. The growth in exports of manufactures was also dominated by a small group of countries, three of them supplying 40 per cent of the total and ten of them 75 per cent in 1978.[8]

1.22   It would be a mistake, however to suppose either that this changing structure of exports or the question of market access for manufactures relates only to a handful of developing countries. Many other oil-importing developing countries are experiencing similar increases in the share of processed and manufactured products in their total export receipts. 'Latecomers' in this respect can expect to move into industrial exporting activities which the 'firstcomers' vacate as they continue to industrialise. Even those countries which rely overwhelmingly upon primary product exports can usually make semi-processed and processed versions of them as their development proceeds.

1.23   Oil-importing developing countries that are still mainly dependent on a limited range of exports of primary products — and this includes most of the least developed countries — have had to face both a slower expansion in world markets and declining terms of trade over the past decade. In 1980 the low-income oil-importers were exporting 42 per cent more by volume than in 1970 but their purchasing power over imports (net of fuel imports) was almost one-third lower than in 1970.[9]

1.24   The change in the terms of trade against the oil-importing countries has become increasingly pronounced over the past eighteen months. In that period the dollar price of their commodity exports has fallen on average by nearly one-third. Primary commodities other than oil may now purchase less in real terms (per unit of export) than they have done at any time since the Second World War.[10] The effects upon the developing countries that are dependent on exports of primary produce, particularly the poorest who have the least access to means of financing balance of payments deficits and the least flexibility of adjustment, have been severe. Per capita income has actually declined in the majority of the poorest developing countries during the past two years, and there is little immediate prospect of a turnaround.

1.25   The fall in commodity prices has aggravated the chronic balance of payments problems of the oil-importing developing countries. As a group they have been running large current account deficits for several years and have been obliged to borrow heavily to help cover these deficits. Those low-income countries that have been unable to obtain commercial credit have been forced to reduce drastically their investment and consumption expenditures. Many others have incurred a high external debt, a large proportion of which has been contracted on short-term and at high rates of interest. They have to allocate a large and rising proportion of their earnings of foreign exchange to meet the service on that debt. The external debt of middle-income primary producers, for example, rose from 17 per cent of their GDP in 1973 to over 24 per cent in 1980, while their debt service payments as a proportion of export earnings doubled from 10 to 20 per cent. For all developing countries, once repayments of short-term debt are included, the cash flow on debt service absorbed one-half of current account receipts in 1981 compared with one-third in 1977.[11]

The Outlook for Developing Countries' Trade

1.26   There is a marked contrast between some of the expansionary longer-term trends that we have described in the trade of the developing countries and the unpromising immediate prospects now facing them if the present depression continues. Most of the developing countries have come a long way over the past three decades. Where an average growth rate in GDP of 3 per cent per annum seemed ambitious as recently as 1950, a rate of 5 or even 6 per cent was clearly feasible twenty years later.[12] The trade of the developing countries was growing fast until recently and in the past two decades has undergone a major change in structure. Where these countries tended to be heavily dependent on a few staple commodity exports (or even a single one) with volatile prices, a large number of them were beginning to gain a foothold in markets with very different characteristics, where prices are relatively stable and the total market is immense. Except in Africa or among the members of OPEC, fewer and fewer developing countries now depend on a single export for half their earnings of foreign exchange.[13] This diversification could materially reduce the uncertainties attaching to their export prospects and offer new opportunities of long-run growth.

1.27   As a group, the developing countries had begun to make rapid headway in world markets for manufactures and several of them were poised for a more broadly based expansion.[14] Given access to world markets, the developing countries could be expected to take advantage of market opportunities and continue to increase their shares of world trade. At present, this share is still small. In 1980 only 9 per cent of imports of manufactures into developed countries came from developing countries and their share of the market in the developed countries was on the average about 3 per cent. Nevertheless, many of them have become newly alive to the advantages of export-propelled growth and are increasingly ready to adopt policies encouraging it.

13

1.28   On the other hand, the immediate outlook for the trade of the developing countries gives grounds for serious concern. First of all, many of the favourable circumstances from which they profited in the 1970s have disappeared or are much less propitious. Markets in the OPEC countries are no longer booming as they did and remittances by foreign workers in these countries to their home base have ceased to expand. The banks are much less ready to make credit available and the bill to be paid in interest charges is much more formidable. The terms of trade are swinging against the developing countries. All this comes on top of a major change in the economic climate and a devastating slowdown in economic activity throughout the world. This not only contracts the markets in the industrial countries that have been the mainspring of world economic growth but blurs the market signals to which investment responds, so that the developing countries are at a loss to decide which way to turn in planning the future of their economies.

1.29   To make matters worse, the expansionary trends which we discussed earlier are contingent on a freedom of access to markets in the industrial countries that has been steadily curtailed. These trends cannot continue, even if world expansion is soon resumed, unless the drift to protectionism is arrested and reversed. There is a very real danger that protectionism and world depression may feed on one another.

1.30   The trade restrictions that have been introduced over the past decade bear especially heavily on the exports of the developing countries. The new barriers to trade that have grown up in the industrial countries apply with special force to the manufactured exports of those countries and are highly discriminatory.

1.31   Meanwhile, the restrictions on trade in agricultural products, which have all along been denied any form of international surveillance, continue unabated. Indeed the situation here, too, has deteriorated with the entry on a large scale into the limited international markets for these products of some of the world's highest cost producers whose growing exports have been made possible by subsidies (e.g. restitutions in the EEC). Moreover, the narrowing of world markets for agricultural products, resulting from well-nigh universal protection, makes for the very instability of prices that is advanced as an excuse for protection against low-cost suppliers. This leaves the exporters of primary produce in a highly vulnerable position in the face of a world depression. Liberalisation of trade in agricultural products is therefore of great importance and could benefit a significant number of developing countries.

The Rising Tide of Protectionism

1.32   It is not easy to stem the tide of protectionism in a world in which markets have ceased to expand. The costs of adjustment to a growing volume of imports are more readily shouldered if exports are growing too and if the extinction of one set of jobs can be balanced by fresh job opportunities in an expanding economy. But the rate at which resources can be transferred is limited both by rigidities of all kinds — reluctance to change jobs, problems of re-training, logistic limits to the creation and expansion of business units — and by the dilemmas of macro-economic management in seeking to maintain a steady pressure of demand. These dilemmas may oblige governments to retreat from policies of full employment because of the danger of inflation or an external deficit. Once such a retreat is sounded, governments give ear more readily to demands for protection, either on grounds of market disruption and the higher unemployment in prospect or because the external deficit would be aggravated by continued imports.

1.33   So far, new pressures of this kind have, with important exceptions, largely been held at bay. Where the line has been broken, however, all too often it has been imports from developing countries that have suffered most. Resort to new protectionist measures such as voluntary export restraints and orderly marketing arrangements has been increasing and there are signs of a general weakening of the resolve to maintain an open trading system. As we show in Chapter 4, this weakening seems to be happening when the increase in market penetration in developed countries by manufactured exports from developing countries has already slowed down considerably. Early in the 1970s, when the effects of the Kennedy Round of multilateral trade negotiations were still being felt, market penetration by developing countries, though relatively small, grew rapidly. But in the 1980s, notwithstanding the tariff reductions of the Tokyo Round, manufactured exports face a much tougher regime of non-tariff measures.

Links Between Developed and Developing Countries

1.34   In spite of these obstacles, trade between the developed and developing countries is likely to continue to grow. The developing countries (including the oil exporters) in 1980 took nearly a quarter of the exports of the industrial countries and the latter took 70 per cent of the exports of the developing countries. In manufactures alone, these proportions came rather closer together, at 27 per cent and 58 per cent. More important, the dependence of the industrial countries on the developing countries as a market for their manufactures is increasing. As recently as 1973 the proportion of their exports of manufactures that went to developing countries was not 27 per cent as in 1980 but 19 per cent. It is still increasing. There is, moreover, a large and increasing balance in trade in manufactures in favour of the industrial countries. The excess of exports of manufactures from the industrial to the developing countries grew in the period 1973-80 from $37.7 billion to $168.7 billion. The restrictions on the far smaller imports of manufactures into the industrial countries have to be seen in the context of this imbalance, although in popular discussion they rarely are. As we argue in Chapter 5, it is an illusion to suppose that the growing interchange between developed and developing countries can be arrested or limited in one direction without serious repercussions on the flow in the opposite direction.

1.35   The developing countries face a different problem if they must now reconcile themselves to a slower growth of their main markets — the industrial countries. In order to sustain their rate of growth in exports they need to secure a higher share in a market that is stagnating or contracting. If access to the market is increasingly restricted this intensifies the difficulty. Yet if the momentum of export expansion in the developing countries falters, the pace of development in their domestic economies is also likely to suffer. The question, therefore, arises what options are open to the developing countries in the face of a continuing slow-down in world trade and increased protection in the markets of the industrial countries.

1.36   The first possibility would be to turn to the more rapid expansion of their domestic markets. But these markets, particularly in the smaller countries, can rarely sustain output of manufactures on the scale necessary for efficient production. Where that scale is possible, as in clothing and textiles, the domestic market is usually already adequately supplied. Thus the resources that fail to be absorbed in exports have to be absorbed in other directions where there is likely to be either an existing excess of manpower and capacity, or an inefficient use of resources behind protective barriers.

1.37   A second possibility would be for the developing countries to offer each other preferential access to one another's markets, with a view to building up a "depression-proof" zone less closely dependent on depression-prone markets in the industrial countries. Apart from the problems encountered in the past by a purely regional approach of this kind, there are obvious difficulties in organising such arrangements, such as have been experienced repeatedly in developing countries' attempts at economic cooperation and integration. They would probably look highly favourable to the limited group of newly industrialising countries (NICs) which account for over half the total exports affected. Their success would be highly dependent, however, upon the full cooperation of the oil-exporting countries which account for over a third of the total imports of manufactures into developing countries but are not themselves exporters of manufactures of much importance. In the immediate future, there is the further problem of relative magnitudes. The developing countries in 1980 sold over 50 per cent more in manufactures to the industrial countries than they sold to one another. A lower rate of growth in sales to industrial countries could only be offset by a considerably higher rate of growth in sales to other developing countries.

1.38   Nevertheless, recent experience shows that there is some possibility of more intra-trade providing a larger share of the growth in developing countries' exports. Whereas total sales of manufactures to industrial countries grew between 1973 and 1980 from $15.75 billion to $58.5 billion, i.e. by 270 per cent, sales to other developing countries grew from $6.85 billion to $38 billion, i.e. by 455 per cent. This faster rate of growth occurred in spite of the high levels of protection in most developing countries. A lowering of these barriers by the more advanced and rapidly growing developing countries would seem the most effective way to encourage further expansion in trade between developing countries.

The Wider Effects of Protection

1.39   The damage resulting from restrictions on trade extends far beyond the immediate economic effects considered in this Report. Any limitation of foreign markets has repercussions on the pace of agricultural and industrial development, on structural change and longer-term prospects of growth. When foreign markets are in doubt the mobilisation of capital from domestic and, still more, from foreign sources is impeded and the repayment of outstanding debt may be jeopardized. Above all, resentments may build up and issue in aggressive exchanges and a breakdown of peaceful relations when opportunities of fruitful effort are cut off by arbitrary and discriminatory acts on the part of foreign powers.

References

1. GATT, *International Trade in 1981 and Present Prospects,* Press Release 1313, 23 March 1982, p.13.

2. UNCTAD, *Trade and Development Report, 1981,* p.34. The figures of per capita real income, which take account of changes in the terms of trade, show a rise from 2.4 per cent per annum in the 1960s to 4.5 in the 1970s.

3. *Ibid.,* p.34.

4. All references to dollars in this Report refer to United States dollars except where otherwise specified.

5. UNCTAD, *op.cit.,* p.38.

6. IMF, *World Economic Outlook, 1982,* Appendix B, Table 13, April 1982.

7. GATT, *International Trade 1962,* Table 10, p.28.

8. World Bank, *World Development Report 1981,* p.24.

9. *Ibid.,* p.21.

10. IMF, *op.cit.,* p.137.

11. *Amex Bank Review,* 26 April 1982, p.1.

12. W.A. Lewis, "The Slowing Down of the Engine of Growth", *American Economic Review,* Vol. 70, No.4, September 1980.

13. Whereas for 20 African exporters of primary produce the largest single primary export still accounted for 46 per cent of total exports in 1976-78 compared with 49 per cent in 1960, for 23 non-African exporters of primary produce the fall over the same period was from 46 per cent to 32 per cent, and for a total sample of 56 developing countries from 47 per cent to 36 per cent. (J. Riedel, "Lewis on Trade as the Engine of Growth in Developing Countries", unpublished, 1981).

14. For example, the exports of manufactures of 31 middle-income developing countries (excluding the fast-growing exporters of manufactures), for which particulars are given in the *World Development Report 1981,* increased between 1962 and 1978 from $522 million to $16.1 billion.

2. Malfunction in the Trade Regime: The Growth of Protectionism

" . . . . no new tariff or non-tariff barriers should be erected by industrialised countries against the export trade of any less-developed country in the products identified as of particular interest to the less-developed countries . . . . particularly . . . . barriers of a discriminatory nature."

GATT Programme of Action, 1963

The Changing Environment of World Trade

2.1   Though less comprehensive in its coverage than the proposed International Trade Organization (ITO) for which it substituted, the General Agreement on Tariffs and Trade (GATT) has nevertheless been the central institution in the world trading regime for 35 years. Above all, it was originally designed to encourage the dismantling of the barriers to international trade which had accumulated during the 1930s and the Second World War, and to prevent a relapse into the protectionist excesses of previous periods. The GATT thus found its *raison d'etre* in, and was influenced in the formulation of its operational procedures by, the bitter experience of the immediate past. Since its establishment, world politics, production and trade have evolved in ways that could not have been foreseen. So have governmental policies relating to the areas of traditional GATT concern. To this evolution of world trading conditions and arrangements, the GATT has attempted some adaptations. There is a considerable gap, however, between the international trading regime as it was envisaged in 1947 and the way it now operates.

2.2   The original aspiration of the architects of the GATT was of a world of equally treated and independent trading partners, interacting upon competitive and 'open' markets in a non-discriminatory fashion. Part of this liberal ideal involved multilaterally agreed restraints upon restrictive business practices, as well as upon governmental barriers to trade, but while such provisions were part of the proposed ITO, they were not contained in the GATT. There were also other major gaps (as will be seen) in the translation of the ideal into the practicalities of the Agreement. The assumptions underlying the desire for an open world economy, of liberal and non-discriminatory trade among independent actors in competitive markets, may never have been totally realistic. In any case, they are now open to challenge in significant respects.

2.3   The rapid growth in world production and trade from the late 1940s to the early 1970s was accompanied by a significant transnationalisation of corporate economic activity. The revolution in communications technology and the liberalisation of exchange controls offered new encouragement to 'international production' through the vehicle of direct foreign investment. Scale-economies, not only in production but also in management, marketing, finance, and information systems, further encouraged the growth of large transnational firms. These developments were associated with growth in international trade in invisibles — factor and non-factor services paid for by royalties, fees, interest and profit. They also produced a significant expansion in international intra-firm trade, which now accounts for somewhere between 25 and 50 per cent, depending on definitional differences, of trade among member countries of the Organisation for Economic Cooperation and Development (OECD). This trade is more predictable and less susceptible to the conventional forces of the arms-length free market. In the short-run, it can be regarded as 'administered' trade, with potential for practices which are restrictive or otherwise not in the social interest of one or the other trading partner. On the other hand, intra-firm trade may also be effectively 'managed' so as to ease a particular firm's or industry's adjustments to longer-run changes; and the firms engaging in it may be potent forces against governmental trade 'management'.

2.4   The GATT is silent on restrictive business practices, direct foreign investment and intra-firm trade. Such international discussion as there has been on these matters has therefore taken place in other fora such as OECD and the United Nations Conference on Trade and Development (UNCTAD). The link between trade in goods and services and international investment decisions has become so important, however, that it is difficult today to discuss one in isolation from the other. The trading environment has become an important new element in investment decisions, particularly those which are geared toward exporting.

2.5   Another aspect of the post-war period has been the unprecedented pace of technical change and the growing perception on the part of OECD governments that comparative advantage can to some degree be created via investments in research and development. High-technology producer goods (and military equipment) are now matters of intense governmental interest and encouragement. The role of international price competition in their development and supply has thus been greatly reduced. To some degree this is also true of such goods as optical and photographic equipment, and consumer electronics. Governments now compete in their support for private or state-owned 'national champions' on the technological frontiers of many industries. At the same time they restrict the export of technology to potential competitors in order to protect national advantages.

2.6   The most dramatic increases in intra-OECD trade, in the 1960s and subsequently, were realised through intra-industry exchange; in this kind of trade, differentiated products of the same general type are exchanged on the basis of their differing characteristics rather than merely on that of price, with the result that exports can expand together with imports within the same industry and adjustment problems can thereby be minimised. There is evidence of the growth of this kind of trade among some developing countries as well, e.g. within the ASEAN. Developing country exports of manufactured products to the developed countries are frequently said to be more 'disruptive' than others, in the sense that they typically involve the need for inter-industry rather than intra-industry adjustment. To the extent that labour and capital are less mobile between industries than within them, these exports may create a more demanding test of the developed countries' adherence to the original GATT precepts.

2.7   The governmental role in international trade has by no means been confined to high-technology sectors. Even outside the state-trading countries, some of which are contracting parties in the GATT, significant proportions of international trade in recent decades have become 'administered' by state-traders. Over 40 per cent of US imports and over 30 per cent of US exports involve transactions with foreign firms which are state-owned or state-controlled. This degree of governmental involvement in international trade was certainly not part of the original GATT vision. At the same time, governments typically are far more protectionist and nationalistic in their procurement policies than is the private sector.

2.8   Increasing attention has also been directed to the fact that the industrial countries are fast becoming service economies. International trade in services, broadly defined, rose nearly three times as quickly as trade in goods in the 1970s. Some governments have demonstrated a keen interest in 'managing' parts of this trade. Yet the GATT makes no explicit provision for governmental practices in restraint of trade in services.

2.9   As the world has grown smaller and more interdependent, the international implications of national policies have increasingly become matters of international dispute. Whereas domestic agricultural policies were considered legitimate grounds for exceptions to GATT rules in the original articles of agreement, there were no equivalent provisions relating to domestic industrial or regional or environmental policies. As the latter types of domestic policies emerged as matters of increasing governmental concern, the temptation was to subordinate international obligations to the needs of domestic policies (the practice specifically authorised in the GATT in respect of the agricultural sector). In most instances, i.e. those not involving tariffs or quantitative restrictions, this meant no formal breach of the GATT since it had no rules governing appropriate practices in these respects. National industrial and regional policies have now become important sources of non-tariff interventions in international trade. As will be seen, overtly protectionist non-tariff measures have also proliferated in defiance or evasion of established GATT norms.

2.10   The original multilateral and non-discriminatory GATT model has also been buffeted by the realities of emerging political relationships. The EEC and some of its trading partners have created discriminatory arrangements in favour of one another which, whatever their other effects, are not in the original spirit of the GATT. So have other trading blocs, not least that of the centrally planned economies. The proportion of world trade taking place on the basis of the GATT's m.f.n. tariffs is consequently much lower than was envisaged or intended and is now estimated at no more than 65 per cent. The proportion taking place between independent private actors on an m.f.n. basis would be much smaller. At the same time, close and exclusive working relationships — including the formulation of codes and guidelines governing restrictive business practices and transnational corporate activity — have been developed within the OECD, to relate only to OECD activities, independently of parallel activity under UN auspices.

2.11   Not the least of the new political realities, and the one to which we shall direct the most attention, has been the emergence of the developing countries as independent and increasingly important participants in the world economy. While their pressure has led to special preferential arrangements on their behalf in some parts of the world trading system (see Chapter 6), their 'low-cost' manufactures have been treated at the same time as peculiarly threatening, requiring discriminatory treatment of the reverse kind in other parts of the system; in one way or another, these countries have not been treated as equal trading partners. Their dissatisfaction with the existing institutional machinery in the sphere of international trade has also led to the establishment of UNCTAD whose activities in many respects parallel those of the GATT. UNCTAD was the forum within which a generalized system of preferences for developing countries was developed. It has also developed a multilaterally agreed set of principles and rules governing restrictive business practices, has been particularly active in the sphere of international commodity agreements, and has recently stepped up its research and monitoring of protectionist practices.

The GATT System

2.12 Despite major changes in the environment of world trade, and major gaps in its own capacities, the GATT remains the key multilateral institution in the trading system. The GATT has served as a forum within which trade negotiations are conducted, as the source of the basic principles governing trade policy, and as a centre for the settlement of trade disputes. Its greatest success has been in the gradual reduction of tariff barriers. Over the post-war period, seven rounds of multilateral trade negotiations under GATT auspices brought about a much more open world trading system and thereby contributed in an important way to post-war prosperity.

2.13 Originally these tariff cuts were achieved through bilateral bargaining with the results unconditionally extended, on the principle of non-discrimination, to all others, typically including those who were not even contracting parties to the GATT. In the last two multilateral bargaining rounds (the Kennedy Round of 1964-67 and the Tokyo Round of 1973-79) tariffs were cut on the basis of a negotiated across-the-board formula, from which exceptions were bargained. Inevitably the most important bargains tended to be struck among the major trading nations. Smaller countries, while offered the potential benefits of the major countries' reciprocal deals, did not have their own direct needs fairly and adequately addressed in these tariff-cutting arrangements. Tariff cuts were proportionately greater on products traded among the nations of the OECD than they were on those originating in developing countries. In particular, tariffs in the developed countries remained relatively high on comparatively low skill labour-intensive products, e.g. garments and footwear; and tariff escalation in the processing of primary products continued to generate very high rates of effective protection for developed countries' processing industries.

2.14 As tariff protection gradually declined, albeit with a significant variation from industry to industry, the salience of a variety of non-tariff barriers to international trade increased. The most obvious of these non-tariff instruments are quantitative import restrictions, for which certain provisions had been made in the articles of the GATT. In certain strictly limited circumstances they were originally permissible for agricultural protection, balance of payments purposes, assistance to development in developing countries, and as a safeguard against unforeseen consequences of negotiated tariff cuts. In all circumstances they were to be imposed in such a way as to preserve the cardinal GATT principle of non-discrimination. The GATT also provided for waivers of any of these or other provisions in "exceptional circumstances".

2.15 Non-tariff measures have emerged as a major challenge to the entire GATT system because of: (i) the increased utilisation of formally permissible instruments of non-tariff protection, to the point where the spirit of the original agreement is called into question; (ii) the increasing extent to which these measures have become discriminatory (or selective) in their application; and (iii) the increasing resort to new measures which were not envisaged at the time of the original GATT and for which there are consequently no rules or guidelines.

1. Utilisation of Non-Tariff Measures within the GATT

2.16 The most striking instance of the growing importance of non-tariff protection which is not formally in conflict with the GATT is in the agricultural sector. On the insistence of the United States, quantitative import restrictions were permitted under the GATT when domestic production of the restricted goods was itself controlled or in surplus. Many other developed countries also took advantage of this exception to the prohibition of the use of import controls, to favour their agriculture. In addition, the most important waiver of GATT rules, though originally limited in time, has become more or less permanent. It has fairly been claimed that the developed countries have utilised the GATT to give a semblance of international legal authority to the trade restrictions which have buttressed their protection of domestic agriculture.

2.17 Agricultural protection has a long history and its proponents have justified it on grounds of national security, farm income stabilisation, environmental and other grounds. Over time, however, the developed countries have been expanding their commitments to their agricultural producers. From original objectives and practices of farm price and income stabilisation and insurance against food emergencies, they have generally shifted to systems of high guaranteed prices and rising self-sufficiency, regardless of cost or efficiency.

2.18 The expanding commitment of many developed countries to protect agriculture has necessitated ever more potent instruments of control at the

24

borders. While Japan still protects its agricultural sector by high tariffs, the EEC has adopted the variable import levy and the variable export subsidy. The former permits the landed cost of any imported produce subject to the levy to be raised up to, or above, the level of the domestic support price. It is a simple, powerful and flexible measure which negates comparative advantage. The variable export subsidy permits high-cost domestic surpluses to be exported at prices low enough to compete with commercial supplies from the lowest cost regular exporters to any third market. (Export subsidies were prohibited under the GATT except for primary products, including agricultural ones. In the case of primary products, contracting parties were to avoid export subsidies which would result in their acquiring more than an 'equitable' share of world trade. The interpretation of this provision has become a matter of dispute between the EEC and the United States.) The existence of such complete border protection has effectively delinked domestic prices from international prices, making it possible to raise domestic prices to high levels.

2.19   In the United States, Canada and Japan, the protective agricultural systems have included measures to curtail the production of surpluses of major cereals and some other commodities. But the EEC has for two decades supported farm production growth at rates that greatly exceed consumption growth, even at self-sufficiency levels approaching or exceeding 100 per cent. The inevitable surplus stocks have reached proportions that are very considerable in relation to the volume of world trade, especially for butter, milk powder, wheat, sugar and beef. The United States and, to a lesser extent, Canada have also accumulated large surpluses of some milk products.

2.20   As a result, there is hardly a major agricultural product in which developed countries compete with developing countries, for which the world market is not undermined or distorted by subsidised exports or concessional sales from surplus stocks of developed countries. Subsidised or concessional exports are on offer from developed countries to importers of wheat, barley, maize, rice, sugar, oilseeds and vegetable oils, dairy products, beef and lamb. In some cases, as a consequence of rising agricultural protection, countries which were once large importers have become large subsidised exporters. In 1981, for instance, the EEC became the world's second largest exporter of sugar after Cuba, and of beef after Australia. When subsidised exports over-supply the available markets, it is ironically the exporters with comparative advantage, mainly developing countries, but also Australia for sugar and beef, and New Zealand for dairy products, that usually are forced to adjust, because they cannot afford the large-scale competitive subsidisation of major exports.

25

2. Discrimination within the GATT

2.21   The most significant single breach in the GATT principle of non-discrimination was the set of arrangements developed, within the GATT, to handle the adjustment problems of the textile and clothing industries. These industries are among the most important to developing countries at early stages of industrialisation. This case therefore carries enormous symbolic as well as real economic importance in the developing countries.

2.22   Over 20 years ago, in 1961, the so-called Short-term Arrangements on International Trade in Cotton Textiles were negotiated in GATT to 'regularise' provisions that had been initiated for trade in that sector, involving some breaches (in the form of quantitative restrictions) in the terms of the General Agreement. The difficulties proved to be neither tractable nor transient, and the Short-term Arrangements were converted to the Long-term Arrangements (LTA) in the following year. These Arrangements were renewed in 1967, as part of the Kennedy Round package of agreements, and renewed again in 1970. In 1973, they were replaced by a broader scheme known as the Multifibre Arrangement (MFA) because it relates to textiles and clothing of wool and man-made fibres as well as of cotton. This Arrangement effectively removed the main problems of the textiles sector of developed/developing country trade from the Tokyo Round of multilateral trade negotiations. The MFA has since been extended twice, with interpretative protocols, most recently in December 1981.

2.23   All these Arrangements, negotiated under the auspices of the GATT, are 'umbrella' schemes, under which member governments are authorised to negotiate bilaterally for quotas outside the relevant provisions of the GATT Articles (XI to XIII). The LTA and MFA were intended to be temporary, and to allow time for an orderly adjustment of markets and production facilities in the face of mounting supplies from 'low-cost' countries. The realistic political alternative in the circumstances of the time was seen not as free trade, but as unregulated, unco-ordinated and disorderly bilateral restrictions in defiance of the GATT. The authorised non-tariff barriers were explicitly discriminatory — not against developing countries as such, but against 'low-cost' suppliers, of which Japan was the chief at the start of the LTA. Even so, the LTA and MFA stood the GATT on its head, so far as developing countries were concerned, because of the discrimination against them and the dominance of this sector in their exports to the developed countries. For this reason, for them, the GATT came to represent protection and discrimination rather than the liberalisation and non-discrimination on which it had tended to pride itself.

3. New Non-Tariff Measures

2.24   Non-tariff measures of many other kinds have increasingly been deployed by governments to restrict the free flow of international trade in circumstances in which they are "bound" by their GATT or other commitments not to employ tariffs. Orderly marketing arrangements (OMAs) of the MFA type are only the most visible. In order to circumvent the obligations of Article XIX of the GATT (viz. prior consultations, non-discrimination, and compensation for resulting losses to those affected) which concern the imposition of restrictions on imports which cause or threaten "serious injury", there has been increasing resort to bilaterally negotiated 'voluntary' export restraints (VERs) in many sectors other than textiles and clothing, e.g. footwear, television sets, steel, motor vehicles, etc. These 'self-imposed' export restraints are agreed against the backdrop of the threat of more severe protectionist measures imposed unilaterally by the importing countries. They are typically not subject to the approval of parliaments, as are tariffs; indeed, they are frequently not even in the public domain.

2.25   There is nothing new about OMAs and VERs in themselves. These forms of protection were used much earlier and a good deal more thoroughly in agriculture than they are now in industry. What is new is the scale of such 'administered' trade. According to one source,[1] about 40 per cent of trade by all market economy countries was 'managed' before 1974; by 1980 this had risen to just under half. Most of the trade in non-manufactures was already managed in 1974, and the rise since then has been small. In manufactures, however, the managed share has risen from 13 per cent to almost a quarter.

2.26   What is of particular concern in the LTA and MFA experience, and in the new OMAs and VERs, is the continued temporal extension of arrangements intended at first to be short-term, the steady broadening of product coverage to keep pace with the development of technology, the extensive broadening of country coverage to stem circumvention by transfer of technology, capital and management to new locations and, more recently, the tightening of restrictions on products and exporting countries that have achieved marked import penetration. Whether reversible or not, the drift of events has been steadily away from the Article XIX[2] concept of temporary and narrowly defined protection toward wholesale sectoral regulation of markets. These OMAs, using VERs and undertaken in quantitative terms, may, it is widely feared, come to typify much of developing/developed country trade.

2.27   There have been so many new instruments of governmental protection in the 1970s that the phenomenon of their growth has spawned a term for them — the "new protectionism". Typically, the "new" instruments are employed in defence of particular industries; and often for the benefit of particular firms. In addition to quotas, OMAs and VERs, they concern such aspects as governmental procurement policies; local content requirements; laws regarding health, safety, sanitary or other standards; discretionary licensing; variable import levies; and explicit or indirect subsidies to national or foreign firms, sometimes under the guise of "industrial policies". Anti-dumping and countervailing duties are also increasingly prominent. So are direct and indirect export subsidies. Increasing proportions of international trade are now subject to regulation or administration, and thus to discretionary decision-making rather than to pre-agreed rules or relatively automatic devices such as traditional import tariffs. Discretionary decisions, where they relate to principles at all, are made with reference to a maze of new legal terms of rather fuzzy economic content — "serious injury", "material injury" or the risk thereof, "market disruption", "unfair" or "low-cost" competition, "minimum viable production", etc. This relative breakdown of order and automaticity is usually accompanied by *de facto* discrimination among trading partners.

2.28   A number of attempts have been made to draw up an inventory of all of the new forms of trade protection. The GATT, for instance, has a list of over 600 different types of non-tariff measures. A precise quantification of the extent of their utilisation is impossible. Apart from the fact that trade restrictions cannot simply be added up, there are difficulties both of definition and access to information. Definitional problems involve questions not only of legality (in terms of GATT) but also of motivation, since trade effects of national policies are frequently incidental and sometimes unintentional. Access to information presents an especially difficult problem in the case of informal arrangements, government deals with particular firms, and intra-firm practices.

2.29   The new protectionism is by no means exclusively directed against the products of developing countries, although that has been its general bias. Trade disputes among the developed countries over the use of new protectionist instruments have also been growing in their frequency and intensity. Particularly acrimonious have been those between Japan and certain other countries in such sectors as motor vehicles, shipbuilding, steel and consumer electronics. The United States and the EEC have also recently deployed new protectionist instruments against one another in the steel and agricultural sectors. These disputes among the major developed countries attract more attention because of the relative equality and bargaining capacity of the protagonists. The damage more quietly done to developing countries' trade by the new protectionist barriers of the developed countries is nevertheless of greater overall consequence, particularly in the light of the limited prospect of restraining them through retaliatory measures.

The Tokyo Round

2.30   The last GATT bargaining round — the Tokyo Round — was completed in 1979 and its results are being implemented. It succeeded once again in achieving significant tariff cuts and, once again, these cuts were appreciably lower for the products of greatest interest to developing countries. This Round was originally far more ambitious than its predecessors in that much more than tariff-cutting was prescribed for it.

2.31   At the outset the Tokyo Declaration[3] announced an intention to consider the 'framework' of trade (i.e. the structure of the GATT itself). It also sought to provide "a better balance as between developed and developing countries" in the sharing of the advantages resulting from the expansion of international trade. Specifically, it was intended to apply "differential measures to developing countries in ways which will provide special and more favourable treatment for them in areas of the negotiation where this was feasible and appropriate". The results did not live up to these ambitions and expectations. Perhaps in part because of the oil price shock and the recession, elements of the intended package could not in practice be agreed.

2.32   While average tariffs on industrial products were reduced by about one-third on an import-weighted basis, the reduction for developing country products was only about one-quarter on base levels which were already significantly higher. The minimal progress made in liberalising agricultural trade and the fact that quantitative restrictions under VERs and OMAs were not considered, reduced the significance of the Round still further for developing countries. Some liberalisation was achieved on 'non-competing' agricultural products — certain tropical products — although the effects on the degree of tariff escalation, on which previous Rounds produced little or no progress, were mixed. Some of the consequences of the Tokyo Round concessions on products of interest to developing countries are discussed in Chapter 3.

2.33   One important advance made in the Round was the negotiation of several agreements (codes) on non-tariff measures to improve the rules and provide more effective discipline in the application of these measures. Agreements were concluded on (i) Subsidies and Countervailing Duties, (ii) Technical Barriers to Trade, (iii) Import Licensing Procedures, (iv) Government Procurement, (v) Customs Valuation, and (vi) a Revised

Anti-Dumping Code. These codes were the chief distinguishing feature of the Tokyo Round as compared with previous rounds of multilateral trade negotiations. Some of their characteristics and major limitations are referred to in Chapter 7. With the exception of these codes, which were intended only to begin to introduce greater order by making procedures less arbitrary, more transparent and more uniform, the Tokyo Round failed to make a significant impact on the recognised shortcomings of the system. Although the codes make some provision for favourable treatment of developing countries, they do not go far enough in reflecting the interests of these countries, which in consequence have been reluctant to become signatories (see Chapter 7).

2.34   A further advance for the developing countries was an Enabling Clause legitimising "differential and more favourable treatment" for them. Linked with this legitimation, at the insistence of the developed countries, is agreement to adopt the principle of "graduation" under which such treatment could be subject to periodic review.

2.35   A major failure of the Tokyo Round was its inability to agree upon a new and more effective international safeguards system. Such a system would greatly benefit developing countries in helping to ensure that emergency protection is introduced only on a temporary basis, under international surveillance and for the legitimate purpose of averting "serious injury", carefully defined. There were early hopes of a reform (i.e. a rewriting) of Article XIX, on safeguards[2], in view of the contracting parties continuing evasion of it and the wholesale adoption of bilateral regulation of trade outside the disciplines of the GATT. These hopes soon gave way to the more modest aim of achieving an interpretative protocol. But it proved impossible to reach agreement even on that because of differences of view as to whether it should be permissible to apply safeguards "selectively", i.e. in a discrimatory fashion.

Preferences for Developing Countries

2.36   The relative disadvantages of developing countries in the emerging international trade regime have been periodically recognised in GATT programmes and the policies of the developed countries but so far without much effect. As early as 1963, the GATT's Programme of Action called for a "standstill" on all trade restrictions applied by industrial countries to exports from developing countries[4]. It also enjoined its members to abolish all restrictions on trade in tropical products, a proposition on which the EEC had some reservations, pleading in that regard the interests of the Yaoundé Convention countries. Attempts to make substantial progress with trade liberalisation in tropical products during the Kennedy Round foundered on the same rock. In the mid-1960s, a new part was added to the

GATT (Part IV) which authorised the granting of non-reciprocal tariff concessions to the developing countries, and absolved them of the requirement of reciprocity[5]. This proved of little practical importance, however, since without reciprocity the developed countries saw no advantage in offering concessions to any trading partners, however deserving, and offered very few; during the Tokyo Round, despite Part IV, some developing countries were specifically adjured by specific developed countries to offer reciprocal concessions to them.

2.37 Although it was not a GATT initiative, the Generalized System of Preferences (GSP) also was created for the special advantage of the developing countries. Preferential access to the markets of the EEC on a more comprehensive basis has also been granted, without reciprocity, under the terms of the Lomé Convention, to a large number of African, Caribbean and Pacific (ACP) countries. The United States now proposes to offer non-reciprocal and preferential market access to a number of countries in the Caribbean Basin. These efforts to develop preferential trading areas between particular developed countries or groups of them, and particular groups of developing countries, as in the Lomé Convention and the proposed Caribbean scheme, are not in the spirit of the original GATT principles of non-discrimination and universality.

2.38 There have also been numerous attempts to stimulate trade among developing countries through preferential schemes. Most have been introduced, with rather mixed success, at the regional level, e.g. the Andean Group, the Central American Common Market, the Caribbean Community, ECOWAS, ASEAN, etc. Some have been more general in their coverage, such as the GATT Protocol Relating to Trade Among Developing Countries which embraces special provisions for a range of commodities and 16 developing countries. For some years efforts have also been made in UNCTAD to develop a general system of trade preferences among developing countries. While there are undoubtedly under-exploited and increasing opportunities for future trade among developing countries, for the present their major markets and trading prospects remain in the industrialised world.

2.39 Some preferential and other special arrangements affecting developing country trade are considered at greater length in Chapter 6. For the present it suffices to say that their importance is dwarfed by the overall changes in protectionist practices and the difficulties being created and expected in future from the malfunctioning of the global trade regime.

Overall Perspective

2.40 International trade today is evidently in large part not governed by the principles and rules formulated by the original negotiators of the

GATT. A high proportion of trade takes place on a basis other than that of unconditional m.f.n. tariffs; discrimination is found both at a general level, as between members of different 'tiers' or trading blocs (the OECD, the EEC etc.) and selectively, in respect of particular countries and industries. There is wholesale abuse or evasion not only of GATT principles but even of prescribed GATT rules, particularly in respect of quantitative restrictions; there is growing resort to non-tariff measures for which there are no GATT rules. Bilateralism has been substituted for the envisaged multilateral approaches to trade negotiation, policy debate and dispute settlement. As non-tariff measures have proliferated, the transparency of trade barriers has been reduced, making monitoring, surveillance and assessment of effects much more difficult. In general much higher proportions of international trade are being 'administered' and 'managed', both by governmental and by private transnational actors, than the original GATT negotiators anticipated. Where discretion replaces rules, the weakest invariably lose most. In consequence of these and other developments there has recently emerged a popular climate of increased legitimacy for protectionist pressures and arguments in the developed countries.

2.41   There has thus been a quantum leap in the degree of uncertainty surrounding market access. This increased uncertainty is bound to inhibit and distort trade and investment. These developments also call into question the credibility of such rules and institutions as have governed international exchange over recent decades. Uncertainties, by influencing trade and investment decisions, generate the very conditions which make for still greater encroachments upon liberalised trade and thus breed further uncertainties in an ever-intensifying downward spiral.

2.42   The new protectionism involves the re-emergence of a very old form of protectionism with its origins in the age of mercantilism. The last great burst of bilateral trading deals, demands for country-specific reciprocity, special arrangements, and managed trade occurred in the 1930s. The bitter lessons learnt from that period were the origin of the GATT principles of multilateralism and non-discrimination, and its attempt to introduce some rules to the international trading jungle. The potential losses to the world trading system from a return to the oldest forms of protectionism are very great. Among the unfortunate, but very real, possible consequences is a renewed inward orientation on the part of developing countries which might seek to protect themselves, singly or collectively, by opting out of expanding trade possibilities with the developed world.

2.43   It is ironic and tragic that a new protectionism should be appearing in the developed countries at a time when there has been a trend toward increasing trade liberalisation and outward orientation in the developing ones, particularly in the newly industrialising countries. In all of the developing countries there is now a more sophisticated awareness of the potential role of external trade in economic development than there was twenty years ago, and a consequent swinging away from previous overly inward orientations of a highly protectionist character. Most developing countries have managed significantly to diversify their exports and to expand their participation in the world economy. The new protectionism, which is in part a response to the developing countries' very success in this respect, risks the loss of the potential for more creative use, both by the developing countries and the world as a whole, of their trading opportunitites.

2.44   The need to bring the growing volume of officially and unofficially 'administered' trade within the purview of GATT, to subject it to international surveillance, to submit it to internationally agreed rules, and to establish a link with industrial adjustment, lie at the heart of the problem of protection as it affects relations between developed and developing countries. The view has been growing in the developed countries that, in a world of 'administered' trade, any country that frames its policies on a presumption of free trade is simply handing over decisions regarding its domestic industrial structure to others. The prevailing conditions of idle industrial capacity and the level of unemployment of labour increase temptations to employ 'easy' protectionist solutions, particularly when they do not breach any agreed international conventions.

2.45   There is undoubtedly some connection between the macro-economic circumstances in particular countries and their attitudes towards import competition. It is much easier to tolerate import pressure and to restructure one's economy as required when one is experiencing rapid economic growth. High unemployment will tend to trigger pressures to preserve jobs by restricting imports. Similarly, balance of payments pressures may generate trade barriers as happened, for instance, in the United States when an across-the-board import surcharge was imposed in August 1971, a measure for which the GATT has no provision. It has become increasingly evident then, that trade policies, however inappropriate to the solution of macro-economic problems, cannot be considered in isolation from monetary, fiscal or exchange rate policies. Nor can the principles and practices of the GATT be totally divorced from those of the International Monetary Fund. The same employment or income objectives can be pursued via numerous alternative mixtures of policies; each policy mix has its own international implications which affect the commodity and geographical composition of trade in its own way.

2.46 Temporary balance of payments pressures, high unemployment and slower growth may help to explain the recent resurgence of protectionist pressures in the developed countries. But, as has been seen, the degree of malfunctioning in the present world trade regime has deeper roots than these. The particular characteristics of current protectionist policy measures suggest that they are the product of more fundamental influences, including changes in world trading patterns and in the way international trade is conducted and perceived. There must therefore be careful consideration of the requirements of an effective international trading and investment order that takes the new realities more satisfactorily into account.

References

1. S.A.B. Page, "The Revival of Protectionism and its Consequences for Europe," *Journal of Common Market Studies,* September 1981.

2. The terms of the present Article XIX are set out in Appendix 2.

3. Declaration agreed at the GATT Ministerial Meeting in Tokyo in September 1973 which formally launched the multilateral trade negotiations.

4. Conclusions of the GATT Ministerial Meeting held in Geneva from 16 to 21 May 1963. (GATT: *Basic Instruments and Selected Documents,* twelfth supplement, June 1964.)

5. The terms of Part IV of the GATT are set out in Appendix 1.

3. The Extent of Protection

"Member States aim to contribute, in the common interest, to the harmonious development of world trade, the progressive abolition of restrictions on international trade and the lowering of customs barriers."

Treaty establishing the European Economic Community, Rome, 25 March 1957

". . . basic objectives shall be to achieve the expansion of trade, the reduction of barriers to such trade and the progressive liberalisation of world trade in textile products. . . ."

GATT Arrangement Regarding International Trade in Textiles (Multifibre Arrangement), 1974

3.1 This chapter examines the nature and intensity of protection as currently applied by the major developed countries. It begins with the primary products which are of basic importance to the economies of many developing countries, particularly the poorer ones, and some developed countries; the focus is primarily upon agricultural products, where the barriers impeding the trade and the development of exporting countries, many of them non-tariff, are greatest. For fuels and minerals in unprocessed form, tariffs are of minor importance, and where other barriers exist, they derive from special conditions of trade in these products. Primary processing, which follows, is a type of manufacturing which merits separate attention because it is in so many cases impeded by the very high effective rates of protection accorded developed countries' processing industries. In the next section on manufactures generally, the whole panoply of 'new protectionist' measures is briefly surveyed. Finally, attention is drawn to the increasingly important trade in services, which is also subject to various restraints, including some unique to that sector, and the special problems of evolving multilateral rules and disciplines in this area are addressed.

I – Primary Products

Competing Agricultural Products

3.2 Protection is most in evidence for products which can be grown in both developed and developing countries. The main commodities concerned are cereals (wheat, coarse grains and rice), sugar, oilseeds and vegetable oils, cotton, tobacco, citrus fruit and livestock products, both meat and dairy. For most of these, the greater part of the world export flow comes from developed countries. However, exports of sugar, rice, cotton, tobacco, beef and vegetable oils are also of great importance to the trade and development of a large number of developing countries.

3.3 World trade in agricultural commodities is — and has been for the fifty years since the end of British free trade — dominated by the policy and ability of the developed countries to protect their agricultural systems, or important sectors of them, from outside competition. This situation has engendered some of the most severe tensions in economic relations between these countries that have arisen since the Second World War.

3.4 Meanwhile, the developing country exporters of the competing products, and the smaller developed country exporters as well, lacking the bargaining strength of the big exporters and developed importers, have seen their trade restricted and their development slowed and distorted by the protectionist policies of the developed countries. To understand the extent of agricultural protection in developed countries it is necessary to quantify its dimensions. Because the nature of the measures applied makes precision difficult, the following assessment uses a variety of approaches.

3.5 Since measures to support and protect agriculture can succeed only if domestic farm prices can be insulated from lower prices offered by foreign suppliers, one indicator of the degree of protection is a comparison of national producer prices. Such a comparison is presented in Table 3.1 for certain major commodities.

3.6 With a producer price almost double that of the main exporters, namely the United States, Canada, Argentina and Australia, the EEC has rapidly become a large exporter of subsidised wheat, with its share of world exports rising from 6 to 14 per cent in the last five years. Thus the EEC's Common Agricultural Policy (CAP) not only imposes a high barrier to imports but also offers subsidised wheat in competition with developed and developing country exporters. The high degree of protection of rice in the industrial countries is evident from a comparison with the situation in the major developing country exporters, Thailand, Burma and Pakistan.

36

TABLE 3.1
Producer Prices in Selected Countries, Average 1977-79
$US per tonne

Wheat		Rice (paddy)			Cattle *a*	Milk *a*
Australia	107	Burma	63	New Zealand	78	8
Canada	111	Pakistan	80	Australia	100	11
Argentina	118	Thailand	131	Argentina	109	—
United States	119	United States	190*b*	United States	199	22
EEC	209	EEC	284	EEC	297	26*b*
Switzerland	517	Japan	1,034	Sweden	335	34
Japan	684			Switzerland	515	38
				Japan	582	51

a Prices per 100 kg. *b* Target price.
Sources: IWC, *World Wheat Statistics,* 1981; FAO, *Committee on Commodity Problems* (CCP: RI 82/7 and CCP: ME 80/4).

Many developing countries export rice to the EEC, subject to import levies ranging during the 1970s from zero to 60 per cent of the EEC entry prices. By far the biggest exporter to the EEC is the United States, a protected supplier. The EEC, Japan and the United States all make subsidised or concessional sales or aid disposals of rice, which is not to the advantage of the low cost developing country exporters. For oilseeds, during recent years US groundnut producers have received prices more than twice those ruling in a major African exporter, Senegal, while the EEC producer price for soya beans has been about three times that of the United States and about four times that of Brazil. Sunflower and olive oil are strongly protected in the EEC, as is rapeseed in the EEC, Finland, Poland, Sweden, Switzerland and Yugoslavia. Because of their highly protected domestic markets, the EEC is the world's largest dairy exporter, the United States has large surplus stocks, and Sweden and Switzerland are subsidised exporters; and the EEC is now the world's second largest exporter of beef, after Australia.

3.7 The available evidence indicates that the present enormously high levels of protection on temperate zone agricultural commodities in various industrial countries are the end result of a rising trend over two or three decades. In addition to comparisons of actual producer prices, another indication of the degree of price support involves the calculation of the percentage by which prices received by domestic producers exceed the prices at which the products are available from foreign suppliers or could

37

be sold to foreign consumers. Using this type of indicator (known as the ad valorem tariff equivalent of protection measures), two Swedish economists[1] calculated that the level of price support in Western Europe, based on prices of wheat, sugar, milk, beef, pork and eggs, had doubled in some countries between 1956-57 and 1968-69; the proportion by which domestic prices exceeded world prices had risen in this period from 36 to 69 per cent for the EEC and from 38 to 62 per cent for Western Europe as a whole.

3.8   For the EEC, the rising trend in the level of protection that occurred in the 1950s and 1960s had not been arrested in the 1970s, as indicated in Table 3.2.

3.9   Dairy production appears as the most heavily protected sector of the European Community's agriculture, but the levels of protection are also high for sugar, wheat, maize and beef. The fluctuations in the indicator levels reflect changes in the external price levels, the degree of protection being low or negative in periods of high world prices, notably in 1973-74 and 1974-75. The nominal levels of the internal EEC prices have been rising virtually continuously. Thus the Community achieved its agricultural policy objective of internal price stability, but also raised the degree of protection for most commodities through the 1970s.

TABLE 3.2
Ad valorem Tariff Equivalents of Agricultural
Protection in the European Community, 1970-71 to 1979-80
per cent above world price

	Butter	Oilseeds	Wheat (soft)	Maize	Sugar (white)	Beef	Rice (husked)
1970-71	381	31	89	41	103	40	110
1971-72	72	47	109	76	45	33	105
1972-73	149	31	53	43	27	12	15
1973-74	220	−23	−21	−2	−34	10	−40
1974-75	216	−20	7	6	−59	62	−19
1975-76	220	27	24	28	9	96	37
1976-77	301	21	104	63	76	92	66
1977-78	288	53	116	103	155	96	28
1978-79	303	61	93	101	176	99	57
1979-80	411	85	63	90	31	104	31

Sources: Eurostat, *Yearbooks of Agricultural Statistics;* Statistical Office of the European Communities.

3.10   Agricultural protection has also shown a long-term rising trend in Japan. Thus the extent by which domestic prices exceeded import prices rose between 1955-59 and 1975-79 from 46 to 256 per cent for grains, soya beans and sugar (as a group), and from 113 to 284 per cent for beef.[2] Calculations made by FAO[3] show definite rising trends for rice, wheat, sugar and beef. In the United States in recent years there has been a tendency towards greater protection for sugar and some livestock products. Further indications of increasing levels of protection in the late seventies in the United States, the EEC and Japan for some important products are provided by FAO estimates of the value of subsidies to producers. In the case of milk there was an increase over the five years 1976-80 from $3.8 billion to $8.1 billion in the United States, from $15.6 billion to $23.1 billion in the EEC, and from $0.3 billion to $0.5 billion in Japan.

3.11   Two commodities, sugar and beef, have been chosen as examples of the way in which growing agricultural protectionism is being applied.

Sugar

3.12   For many decades sugar production has been protected in the major developed market economies, particularly the EEC, Japan and the United States. The EEC adopted a common regime for sugar in July 1968, which supported sugar growers by providing them with higher prices than would under normal circumstances be available on the world market. This was achieved through variable import levies and export subsidies (restitutions). There was also a system of production quotas and an element of producer 'co-responsibility' in the form of a levy on a secondary part of the quota in order that producers should share the costs of surplus production.

3.13   The renewal of the regime in 1974 followed a period of world shortage, the enlargement of the Community and the agreement to import 1.3 million tonnes per annum from ACP countries under the Lomé Convention and from India at prices related to EEC levels. Under this second regime, which operated from 1975 to 1981, the Council of Ministers raised the maximum EEC production quota by a substantial amount, and lifted the support price of sugar to improve its profitability vis-a-vis other CAP products. Provision was also made for a Community stockpile. The margin by which the Community support price (increasing annually) exceeded world sugar prices rose from 9 per cent in 1975-76 to a peak of 176 per cent in 1978-79.

3.14   In this favourable policy environment, Community sugar production grew faster than world production, contributing 16.5 per cent

39

of the latter in 1981-82 compared with 12.7 per cent in 1975-76. Consumption in the Community remained stagnant, and the level of self-sufficiency rose from 91.4 per cent in 1974-75 to 130 per cent in 1979-80. The only outlet for the excess production was the export market. In 1977 the Community changed from a net importer to a net exporter. It stayed outside the International Sugar Agreement, and its share of world exports increased from 8.3 per cent in 1976 to 18.3 per cent in 1981. This expansion was only made possible by export subsidies, and it aggravated the 1981 fall in world prices. The statistical picture of these changes is presented in Table 3.3.

TABLE 3.3
Sugar: World and EEC

	Production (million tonnes, raw value)		Exports a (million tonnes, raw value)		Prices, white sugar (ECU per tonne)	
	World	EEC	World	EEC	World	EEC
1975-76	80.2	10.2	22.8	1.9	293.5	304.5
1976-77	85.5	10.4	28.4	2.7	200.5	331.4
1977-78	91.7	12.2	25.0	3.6	137.6	396.9
1978-79	90.6	12.4	25.9	3.6	128.5	404.9
1979-80	84.2	13.0	26.7	4.3	327.3	410.9
1980-81	87.1	13.0	29.0	5.3	538.8	432.7
1981-82	97.0[b]	16.0[b]			270.0[b]	469.5

a Calendar years (1976-81).
b Estimate.
Sources: FAO; International Sugar Organization; EEC Commission.

3.15 Sugar (and isoglucose) will remain heavily supported in the EEC under the new five year regime that came into operation in July 1981. However, the 'co-responsibility' levies on producers have been increased, and EEC beet plantings are expected to be reduced by 7 per cent in 1982. Since the Community is likely to be holding stocks of over 3 million tonnes at the end of the season, the reduction in plantings will probably have little effect on free market supplies in 1983. The longer-run impact on the EEC and world markets of the larger degree of 'co-responsibility' imposed on producers remains to be seen.

3.16 The impact of the EEC sugar regime on developing countries is complex. While ACP suppliers benefit from preferential access at Community prices, their sales to the free market suffer reduced prices as a result of the Community's subsidised exports. The balance of effects is mainly positive for most ACP suppliers, as long as the preferential access continues and their production for the free market is small and has not been greatly impeded by artificially low world market prices.

3.17   The United States is the largest developed market importer of sugar. In 1980 it ratified the International Sugar Agreement and, owing to the rise in world prices, reduced its variable import duty and determined that a price support programme was not necessary for the 1980 and 1981 crops. But, at the end of 1981, as world prices declined again, a sugar loan programme was re-introduced for the period 1982-85 inclusive, with price support in the form of increased import duties, quotas and fees. The implications of this decision for the world sugar market are potentially serious. It is likely to reduce consumption in the United States, as higher prices encourage an even greater switch to sugar substitutes. Increased domestic production and reduced import demand from the largest free market importer will have depressing effects on world prices and particularly serious implications for Central American and Caribbean countries, some of whose economies depend substantially on sugar exports to the United States.

Beef

3.18   Under the EEC common beef and veal regulations which came into effect in July 1968, support prices have been set which have remained above world prices: some 90-100 per cent above since 1975-1976 (see Table 3.2). The main price support mechanisms are intervention buying at given prices, aid to private storage, a common customs duty, variable import levies, safeguard action (e.g. suspension of imports between July 1974 and March 1977), and refunds on EEC exports outside the Community. In the framework of this highly protective regime, EEC beef production has increased. Since the period of suspension, imports have not recovered to earlier levels, but exports have increased. In 1979, the EEC became a marginal net exporter of bovine meat, and a major net exporter in 1980 and 1981. EEC gross exports increased from 5 per cent of world exports in 1977 and 1978, to 21 per cent in 1980, second only to those of Australia. EEC subsidised exports are going to the USSR, Eastern Europe and a number of developing countries and appear to have displaced exports from Argentina and Uruguay, as well as from Australia and New Zealand. Their large volume must certainly have contributed to the weakness of international beef prices in 1981 and 1982. EEC imports are now practically confined to the amounts specified in concessionary agreements negotiated under GATT or with particular countries, e.g. Yugoslavia, and four African countries, Botswana, Kenya, Madagascar and Swaziland, under the Lomé Convention.

3.19   In the United States and Canada quantitative restrictions are the major method of regulating the market. The United States Meat Import Act of 1964 introduced import quotas on beef and veal (and certain other meats), and these were linked in 1979 to a counter-cyclical formula. However, voluntary export restraints (VERs) negotiated with major suppliers have avoided the need to impose and administer formal import quotas. Both the United States and Canada have committed themselves to maintain certain minimum import levels. The beef market in Japan is heavily protected by customs duties (at 25 per cent), variable levies, quotas, and cumbersome administrative import procedures.

National Agricultural Policies

3.20   Various reasons, including the so-called inherent value of an agrarian society, the security of food supplies, national self-sufficiency or the attainment of environmental objectives, have been advanced in attempts to justify agricultural protectionism. The key issues, however, are politico-economic and concern the stabilisation and improvement of farm incomes and the assurance of preference for national producers. Once agricultural protection gathers momentum in a developed country, there are powerful forces working for its continuance and enhancement.

3.21   From the standpoint of world trade, the most unfortunate feature of developed countries' agricultural protection policies is the almost universal reliance upon support prices to stabilise domestic markets and farmers' incomes. Rigid support prices (more often than not without supply management) are the most damaging to world markets of the various possible approaches for ensuring protection. The setting of the level of support prices tends to become a decision within the political process in which consumers and importers have generally proved no match for the organised pressures of farmers. As a consequence, the prevailing levels of agricultural protection, illustrated in the earlier tables, are usually very high. At such levels conventional tariffs are unable to provide sufficient border regulation of imports. Hence the resort to measures of more direct border control, such as variable import levies, import quotas and VERs, supplemented by the disposal of surpluses through export subsidies which have for long distorted and frustrated agricultural production, trade and development in the world.

3.22   Alternatives are available. The fundamental requirement is to admit that national agricultural policies are at the root of agricultural trade problems. There is reason to suppose that the present levels of protection are often excessive and higher than necessary to achieve desired objectives. Even without questioning national objectives, there is often room for reconsideration of the degree of protection required, and of the nature of the measures to be employed to achieve it.

3.23   At the national policy level the highest priority should attach to the promotion of farm-income stabilisation and support measures that have a minimum disruptive effect on trade. Alternative forms of agricultural support, having less adverse effects on the trade of other countries, include:

(i)   Direct income supplements to groups of farmers disadvantaged, for example, by the smallness of their farms, unfavourable environmental factors or abnormal climatic conditions.
(ii)   Direct payments to farmers to supplement the incomes derived from sales in the open market.
(iii)   Subsidies on the cost of key production inputs purchased by farmers.
(iv)   The fixing of farm prices based on defined conditions of efficiency and productivity — this measure could be combined with those already listed, viz. direct income supplements and subsidised inputs.
(v)   Farm price support schemes limited to a maximum volume of output or linked with other measures of supply management.

Where agricultural support is necessary, forms should be chosen which, in achieving the aims of the country imposing them, occasion the least damage to exporters.

3.24   The possibility of using such measures is well known in developed countries and indeed their economic advantages are often recognised. Some have political drawbacks in that their cost is obvious in national budgets, whereas high administered prices are paid for in the shops by consumers. For these alternative policy measures to be considered seriously a change in political attitudes needs to be brought about. As and when progress is made with the adoption of alternative means of implementing the objectives of agricultural policies, it should become possible to initiate changes towards less trade-restrictive measures at the border, as discussed in the next chapter.

3.25   Such basic progress towards containing and gradually rolling back the still advancing wave of agricultural protectionism in the world could be facilitated by the initiation of a multilateral review of the international impact of national agricultural policies and measures. Such a review must include the participation of all the major developed countries. It would be a major step ahead if the recent OECD findings on this subject[4] were to lead to the establishment of specific procedures for such a review. A desirable objective would be to develop a multilaterally agreed code of principles on agricultural support measures, which would facilitate progress towards greater trade liberalisation.

Implications for International Machinery

3.26   As long as national producer prices for the main agricultural commodities are so widely divergent, any general liberalisation of agricultural trade seems to be out of the question. The most that can be hoped for immediately, while more basic progress is made in national policies, is a standstill on current protection levels, and the negotiation of increments of access, reductions of surpluses and some international agreement on limits to export subsidies.

3.27   Such a breathing space would make it possible to envisage the negotiation of usable interpretations of obscure concepts in the GATT provisions on subsidies, designed to bring this trade-devastating practice more into the open and under more effective international surveillance. In addition, to strengthen the relevance of GATT to agricultural trade problems, serious efforts are needed to bring within its purview the most restrictive trade practices currently in vogue, namely variable import levies and VERs. These devices currently escape the surveillance of GATT.

Agricultural Raw Materials
3.28   Cotton, wool, jute, hard fibres, rubber, and hides and skins are the main items in this group. Apart from wool and hides and, to a lesser extent, cotton and rubber, they are chiefly products of low income, tropical agriculture. The main markets for all are in the industrial countries which, with some exceptions (notably the United States and where there are synthetic substitutes), cannot produce these products. As raw materials for further industrial processing they are not greatly subject to tariffs in importing countries. One of the main problems facing developing country exporters of agricultural raw materials is the escalation of tariffs imposed by the developed countries on exports in processed forms. This escalation, designed to protect the processing industries in the importing countries, is the subject of the next section of this chapter.

Tropical Non-Competing Agricultural Commodities
3.29   Exporters of these products, which include coffee, cocoa, tea, bananas and spices, are almost entirely developing countries, and importers are predominantly developed countries. A large proportion of the trade in raw or relatively unprocessed form has benefited from gradual

liberalisation measures in developed importing countries. These commodities are among the agricultural products for which the European Community grants preferential access to the 63 ACP countries; they also figure in the commodities granted GSP treatment by individual developed countries. Nevertheless a number of barriers remain which are serious handicaps for individual exporting countries with a high degree of dependence on exports of these products. These barriers take the form mainly of import duties, product-specific revenue taxes and in some cases quantitative restrictions.

3.30   Import duties exist, apart from those for revenue purposes, to protect preferred exporters or, when on the processed product, to afford protection to domestic processors. For tropical beverages the effect of duties is significant with respect to imports of coffee. For example, although nearly 40 per cent of all coffee imports by the EEC are from ACP countries and therefore free of duty, this still leaves the greater part of EEC coffee imports subject to duties. The Community imposes duties on all cocoa and cocoa products, but over 80 per cent of imports come in duty-free under the Lomè Convention. For both coffee and cocoa, the main significance of duties appears to be to maintain an advantage for ACP countries over other developing suppliers. Duties are not generally significant for bulk tea. In the case of bananas more than two-thirds of world imports of fresh fruit are duty-free. Supplies to the EEC from ACP countries and dependent territories are duty-free, and Germany (F.R.) also has a large duty-free quota; nevertheless, about a third of European Community imports (one-eighth of world exports) remain dutiable. Even after relaxations obtained in the Tokyo Round, import duties on spices remain significant in certain areas.

3.31   Although the low price elasticity of demand for beverages tempers the effects of internal taxes as obstacles to consumption, the production-specific taxes imposed on tea and coffee in Germany (F.R.) are sufficiently high to be of significance. Some EEC members have undertaken not to increase such taxes. The internal tax on bananas in Italy is levied at a particularly high rate.

3.32   Few quantitative restrictions exist on imports of tea, coffee and cocoa. Import licensing of fresh bananas is applied in France, Italy and the United Kingdom, the main purpose being to provide sheltered markets for preferred suppliers. The complexity of health standards and quality regulations is a handicap to some trades, especially that in spices.

3.33   The developed centrally planned economies take only a very modest proportion of world exports of tropical products, in relation to their population and income levels. Their imports are mostly subject to duties but the main barriers are associated with state-trading practices, foreign currency allocations and domestic pricing policies. The opening up of the markets of these countries would have a significant effect in enlarging world import demand for tropical products.

3.34   The improvements of recent years in liberalising trade in these products should be completed by the removal of the remaining restrictions, both tariff and non-tariff. While the abolition of tariffs on these products may present problems with regard to the loss of preferences, notably those of the ACP countries, the gradual reduction and rationalisation of differential barriers should be accepted as one of the aims of global trade liberalisation. Towards this end there is scope for initiatives from developing as well as developed countries; it should prove possible to negotiate compensatory concessions in cases of loss of preferences.

3.35   The proportion of national revenue of developed countries that is contributed by the remaining duties and taxes specifically on tropical products is so small that their total elimination, in the interests of facilitating the development of the developing exporting countries, can be regarded as a reasonable objective in the developed countries concerned.

Fuels and Minerals
3.36   The primary forms of major fuels and minerals are virtually free of tariff barriers, though limited degrees of tariff protection are accorded to lead, zinc and nickel in the United States. For some fuels and minerals, tariffs tend to escalate with processing, especially in the case of petroleum products, but such barriers to trade as exist are mainly in the form of non-tariff measures.

II – Processed Products

3.37   In this Report, processed products are considered separately from other manufactures because of the special problems posed for developing countries (and other primary producers) by the protection of industrial country processing industries[5].

Tariffs
3.38   Despite the substantial lowering of tariffs by several rounds of multilateral trade negotiations, processing is an economic activity still significantly protected by tariffs. Many primary products face zero or low tariffs. Higher nominal tariffs tend to apply to the processed forms of these products and this means effective rates of protection are higher still,

sometimes over 100 per cent, since the higher tariffs fall largely on the value added in processing.

3.39   Protection accorded to domestic processing industries by this tariff 'escalation' remains a severe trade policy problem for developing countries and those developed countries such as Australia which depend heavily on raw material production. The problem of tariff escalation has been given inadequate attention in multilateral trade negotiations. Although in the Tokyo Round increased attention was given to tropical products, and while this meant that the absolute differences in tariffs on products at different stages in the processing chain were in many cases reduced, the degree of effective protection for processing frequently remained unchanged because percentage reductions were greater for products at the lower stages[6].

3.40   Data on effective protection are sparse. A study based on post-Tokyo nominal tariffs and recent UK input-output co-efficients shows significant rates of effective protection for the following products in the EEC: 70, 53 and 75 per cent for cocoa liquor, butter and powder, respectively; 28 and 48 per cent for processed coconut oil (for industrial and edible use); and 6 and 21 per cent for truck tyres, and canvas and rubber footwear[7]. More comprehensive estimates based on pre-Tokyo Round m.f.n. tariffs are available. Since the situation has not changed significantly since then, these data remain indicative of the high levels of effective protection of processing activities in developed countries. They are shown in Table 3.4 for products of special interest to developing countries.

3.41   A disturbing aspect of the incidence of tariff escalation is that effective protection tends to be higher in industries in which developing countries are more likely to have comparative advantage. The highest barriers are in industries based on vegetable oils and oilseeds, cocoa, coffee, fibres, hides and skins, and timber.

3.42   The high levels of protection indicated by Table 3.4 are alleviated to some extent by the preferential arrangements which are discussed in Chapter 6. In this connection, the Lomé Convention is of great significance since it provides duty-free and quota-free entry for nearly all processed products exported by the ACP. The GSP is much less important in alleviating protection. GSP rates do not necessarily lead to lower effective rates of protection. In the EEC, in the case of refined coconut oils, effective rates are higher under the GSP than under the m.f.n. Some important processed exports from developing countries are not included, e.g. plywood in the United States and Japanese schemes and refined palm

TABLE 3.4

**Comparison of Nominal and Effective Protection for
Selected Processed Products — Pre-Tokyo Round m.f.n. rates**

	EEC		Japan		United States	
	Nominal	Effective	Nominal	Effective	Nominal	Effective
	%		%		%	
Meat products	19.5	32.6	17.9	69.1	5.9	10.3
Roasted coffee	15.2	35.7	35.0	137.1	0.0	0.0
Cocoa powder						
and butter	13.6	76.0	15.0	125.0	2.6	22.0
Coconut oil	11.5	132.9	9.0	49.2	9.4	16.3
Palm kernel oil	10.5	141.5	7.2	49.2	3.8	29.2
Jute fabrics	19.6	53.3	20.0	54.4	0.0	–0.6
Wood products	8.7	16.3	11.5	23.2	6.7	13.6
Leather	4.8	12.3	11.6	34.7	4.7	12.0

Source: UNCTAD, *The Processing Before Export of Primary
  Commodities: Areas for Further International Co-operation,*
  May 1979.

oil in the EEC scheme. But even where products are included, the uncertainty introduced by the unilateral and non-contractual nature of the concessions, and by the limitations imposed through the ceilings and tariff quotas of the EEC and Japanese schemes and the 'competitive need' criteria of the United States scheme, considerably reduces the significance of the GSP.

3.43   In the case of mineral products, tariffs tend to escalate with the degree of processing. However, levels of effective protection tend on the whole not to be as severe a problem as in the case of agricultural products.

Non-Tariff Measures
3.44   Non-tariff measures (NTMs), such as quantitative import restrictions, licensing procedures, public and quasi-public procurement, and quality standards and packaging regulations, on imports from developing countries, are usually more severe on processed products than on primary products[8]. Trade losses due to these measures may be considerable. Moreover, NTMs are applied most frequently to the products in which poor countries are developing a comparative advantage.

3.45   Among the most costly NTMs to the developing countries are those in the fibre sector, notably in the MFA which is discussed in the next section; these accentuate the protection provided by tariff escalation.

Outside the MFA, sisal products are restricted by VERs. Japan uses NTMs to protect local sugar refiners and the variable levies under the EEC sugar regime thwart the import of processed fruit and chocolate with significant sugar content. Deficiency payments and production aids given to agricultural products deter imports of processed products, as domestic processing industries benefit from the availability of cheap raw materials. Mineral processing is also to some extent affected by NTMs, e.g. minimum import prices.

Potential for Increased Processing
3.46   Trade barriers against the export of processed products from developing countries reinforce historical and other factors, e.g. scarcity of capital, management, skills and technology, which have militated against developing countries undertaking much processing of domestic raw materials.

3.47   In spite of these problems, developing countries have made some headway in establishing processing industries. For a number of products, the proportion of exports sold in raw or near-raw form has declined significantly. Some examples are cocoa, cotton, vegetable oilseeds and oil, fibres, hides and skins, wood products and iron. Greater progress could be made if protection were relaxed. There are many industries where because of factors such as labour intensity, high transportation costs for the raw product, high energy requirements and environmental costs, comparative advantage already exists in developing countries; the removal of tariff and non-tariff barriers would greatly facilitate their development in these countries. An indication of the impact of protection on trade patterns is provided by the case of the coconut oil industry; in the EEC, because of protection to crushers, the import of copra is still significant, whereas in the United States, which offers no such protection, imports are wholly in the form of oil.

3.48   Several studies have indicated high potential for increased export earnings by developing countries through expanded processing of their raw materials and foodstuffs (see, e.g., paragraph 4.16). According to one study, if developing countries undertook additional processing in seven major mineral industries only up to the metal bar stage, they could earn from exports an additional gross $44 billion per annum[9].

3.49   The relaxation of protection could have a significant long-run impact on development and could greatly benefit those low-income raw material producing countries that are not yet in a position to export labour intensive manufactures. Trade barriers which impede processing activities in developing countries should be completely removed. As a start, consideration should be given to the elimination of tariff escalation on processed products for which raw materials emanate largely from the developing countries.

III – Manufactures

3.50   The success of the GATT in reducing industrial tariffs has largely removed the tariff weapon from the hands of the developed countries, which have recently become increasingly concerned to protect certain manufacturing sectors from a surge of exports from Japan and a number of rapidly advancing developing countries. The developed countries are therefore resorting to the same wide range of NTMs to protect important sectors of their manufacturing as they introduced in earlier decades to protect agriculture.

Tariffs
3.51   The reductions in developed country tariffs on manufactures, though wide-ranging, have not covered all products; nor have they been uniform in depth, and by 1 January 1987, after conclusion of the Tokyo Round reductions, the m.f.n. rates in the nine major markets of these countries[10] will still average 10 per cent of more for textiles and clothing and for finished manufactures in the leather, rubber, footwear and travel goods group of products (see Table 3.5).   These two product groups contain goods in whose production the developing countries' comparative advantage is among the greatest, and the relatively less steep reduction in the Tokyo Round of m.f.n. rates on manufactures 'of interest to developing countries'[11] was a source of dissatisfaction to these countries, which were well aware of the relatively higher base rates from which the cuts on their products are being made.

3.52   As a result, by the time the Tokyo Round cuts have been completed, the differential between the m.f.n. tariff on 'developing country manufactures' (an average of 7.9 per cent in the nine major markets of the developed countries) and that on all manufactures (an average of 5.8 per cent) will have increased. Although the effects of this on the developing countries are somewhat offset by the operation of the Generalized System of Preferences, it is not a trend which is consistent with the spirit of the "special and more favourable treatment" that was to be accorded to developing countries. In future GATT multilateral trade negotiations, tariffs on manufactures 'of interest to developing countries' should be cut more heavily than those on other manufactures.

TABLE 3.5
Major Developed Countries: m.f.n. Tariffs *a*
(percentages)

Product		Depth of cut	Post-Tokyo Round average m.f.n. rates *b*
Textiles and clothing	— total *c*	19	11.8
	— semi-manufactures	22	11.5
	— finished manufactures	19	16.7
Leather, rubber, footwear, travel goods	— total *c*	14	6.3
	— semi-manufactures	35	4.4
	— finished manufactures	11	10.2
Electrical machinery, equipment, goods	— total	34	6.1
Chemicals	— total	38	5.3
	— semi-manufactures	36	5.0
	— finished manufactures	43	6.0
Transport equipment	— total	36	5.0
Non-electric machinery	— total	47	4.1
Base metals	— total *c*	31	2.7
	— semi-manufactures	26	3.2
	— finished manufactures	37	5.9
Wood, pulp, paper, furniture	— total *c*	40	1.7
	— semi-manufactures	38	1.9
	— finished manufactures	41	4.2
Manufactures, n.e.s.	— total	42	5.5

a Countries covered are Austria, Canada, EEC, Finland, Japan, Norway, Sweden, Switzerland and United States.
b To become fully effective not later than 1 January 1987.
c Totals comprise raw materials as well as semi-manufactures and finished manufactures.
Source: GATT, *The Tokyo Round of Multilateral Trade Negotiations*, Vol. II, January 1980.

Non-tariff Measures

3.53   The relative lack of importance of tariffs to trade in most manufacturing sectors has not, however, meant that there has been a commensurate decline in the level of trade barriers. For, as was shown in the previous chapter, there has been a considerable extension of NTMs applying to trade in manufactures; in several major sectors there has also been a marked increase in the severity of these measures, which include 'voluntary export restraints' (VERs) and 'orderly marketing arrangements' (OMAs). Although numerical precision is difficult, one source[12] put the proportion of OECD imports of all manufactures controlled by NTMs at 17 per cent in 1980 compared with only 4 per cent in 1974[13]. For manufactures imported by OECD countries from developing countries the proportion in 1979 was estimated at 30 per cent, compared with only 11 per cent for those imported from other OECD members, a reflection principally of the differing importance to the two groups of countries of trade in textiles and clothing.

3.54   The effects of NTMs have been most marked, both in extent and in severity, for textiles and clothing. Estimates based on quota premia suggest that the tariff equivalents of the quotas in this sector are often considerably greater than the tariffs themselves[14]. Other sectors in which NTMs are important (and in some cases crucial) include steel, footwear, consumer electrical and electronics goods (particularly televisions and audio equipment), motor vehicles, ships and chemicals.

3.55   As indicated in Chapter 2, these NTMs, except for the MFA, are outside the purview of the GATT. Thus, although some progress was made in the Tokyo Round on negotiating codes on NTMs, these did not include disciplines covering VERs and OMAs. It is imperative that further progress be now made in this area, and that VERs, OMAs and other unofficial quantitative restraints, together with the MFA, are brought under greater multilateral control and discipline within improved provisions of Article XIX and of the appropriate codes. It is particularly important that clear indications should be given of the circumstances in which protective action under Article XIX and the codes is justifiable and that such action be specified in scope and time-bound. By such means the growing volume of trade in manufactures which is officially or unofficially administered should be brought under international surveillance and submitted to internationally agreed rules and procedures.

3.56   In the remainder of this section we briefly set out some of the main characteristics of protection in the most important manufacturing sectors involved.

Textiles and Clothing

3.57 Trade in this sector remains highly protected, particularly with respect to imports into developed from developing countries. Reductions in tariffs agreed at the Tokyo Round were well below the overall average for manufactures and the resultant rates are well above average, particularly for clothing[15]. Even so, the quotas operated by developed countries under the MFA since the beginning of 1974 were tightened after the Arrangement was extended by protocol in 1977. Whereas in MFA I (1974-77), the norm for quota increases in restrained products (i.e. products deemed to be causing 'market disruption') was "not less than 6 per cent" annually, in MFA II (1978-81), the clause on "jointly agreed reasonable departures from particular elements in particular cases" permitted lower rates of growth which were, in effect, imposed on exporting countries by importing countries through a series of bilateral negotiations. This was quite contrary to the professed object of the original MFA, one article of which includes a clause enjoining the provision of increased access to participating countries' markets for textile products from developing countries (see paragraph 3.66 below).

3.58 Under the MFA II, the EEC transformed the overall 6 per cent limit on restrained products into a system dividing all products from 'low-cost' suppliers into groups according to their degree of 'sensitivity'. For products in the most 'sensitive' group, accounting for more than three-fifths of EEC imports from these suppliers, the bilaterally agreed quotas for 1977 were cut back severely for Hong Kong, Rep. of Korea and Taiwan,[16] the three largest 'low-cost' suppliers, and thereafter were allowed to rise only by between 0.3 and 4.1 per cent annually. Higher rates were allowed for other groups, especially those containing products in which 'low-cost' suppliers showed little or no comparative advantage and in which their market penetration was consequently low, so that the EEC could claim that it had provided for overall growth of 6 per cent. But there was no significant flexibility for switching quotas between groups or between markets. At least 98 per cent of EEC imports of 'low-cost' textiles and clothing are now covered by quotas.

3.59 The United States in 1978 negotiated bilateral agreements with the three biggest developing country suppliers — Hong Kong, Taiwan and Rep. of Korea — which generally allowed quotas to increase at rates well below the 6 per cent MFA norm, with zero growth in some cases. Originally scheduled to last for five years, the agreements were renegotiated in 1979 and 1980, when by imposing a reduction in flexibility and a cut-back on previously unfilled quotas, the American Administration (under industry pressure) reduced effective market access quite considerably. By the end of

1979, about 85 per cent of US imports of textiles and clothing were controlled through quotas.

3.60 Other developed countries also imposed stricter controls by means of bilateral agreements, and all except Japan and Switzerland now apply quotas or almost prohibitive tariffs. But a country does not have to be a signatory of the MFA to protect its textiles and clothing industry effectively. In Australia, for example, the tariff-quota system in operation was estimated to have provided in 1980/81 a nominal rate of protection of 24 per cent for textiles and 60 per cent for clothing and footwear; the average effective rate in 1977/78 was estimated at 48 per cent for textiles and 140 per cent for clothing and footwear[17].

3.61 MFA III (January 1982-July 1986) contains some elements which are less restrictive than before and others which are capable of being more so. On the one hand, in the list of understandings set out as part of the conclusions of the GATT Textiles Committee meetings (annexed to and an integral part of the extending protocol), there is no reference to ''reasonable departures'' from MFA norms, while there is reference to strengthening the definition of ''market disruption'' and of providing specific factual information on its existence or real risk before safeguard measures can be invoked. On the other hand, there is a new provision for cutting back the quotas of 'dominant' suppliers of particular products under ''mutually acceptable arrangements with regard to flexibility''; there is also a new 'anti-surge' mechanism to deal with difficulties arising from sharp and substantial increases in imports which previously were consistently below restraint levels.[18]

3.62 Any assessment of the extent of protection provided by the new Arrangement must take full account of the ensuing bilateral agreements. It is still too early to come to firm conclusions on these, but from recent negotiations between the EEC and United States and major Asian suppliers, and from the statements made by ministers of OECD countries, the portents do not look promising from the standpoint of trade liberalisation.

3.63 EEC Trade Ministers provided the European Commission with a mandate which allowed for an annual increase in Community imports from MFA signatories, centrally planned economies and preferential countries of a mere one per cent for products in the most 'sensitive' group and for an average of only three per cent for those in the next two groups; in addition, Indian handloom and craft products are to be controlled by quota despite their exclusion from the MFA. Quotas for 'dominant' suppliers — Hong Kong, Rep. of Korea, Taiwan and Macao — will be cut by 10 per cent over the four years 1982-85, with a larger cut in the first half. New agreements by the United States with 'dominant' suppliers have also been very restrictive. That with Hong Kong, for example, provides for annual growth in quotas of a mere 0.5-2.0 per cent; similar agreements have been made with Rep. of Korea and Taiwan.

3.64 Overall, therefore, exports of the group of products which have provided developing countries with their earliest experience of manufacturing are still very strictly regulated by an arrangement, administered by GATT, whose signatories account for the bulk of world trade in the products concerned.[19] The experience of developing countries with the MFA and its related bilaterals — with expanding country and product coverage, diminishing growth provisions, increasing complexity and rigidity, and apparent permanence — is contributing considerably to their growing disillusion with the international trading system as presently constituted and with the growth prospects of outward-oriented development policies.

3.65 It is not difficult for the exporting countries concerned to contrast some of the professed objectives of the MFA with the reality of its achievement. Various aspects can be cited, among which the following are merely examples. First, one may contrast the provision that, save in exceptional circumstances, the annual increase in quotas for products under the restraint should not be less than 6 per cent, with European Commission data showing that during 1977-80, the volume of EEC imports of MFA products from countries with which it had negotiated bilateral agreements rose on average by only 2.5 per cent annually (and by a mere 0.8 per cent for the most 'sensitive' group of products).[20] Not that the EEC's growth of imports was the lowest: in the United States, where protection was even more severe, imports of textiles and clothing from developing countries had risen on average by only 3.7 per cent annually during the 1970s and fell 9 per cent in the last year of the decade. Secondly, one may contrast the MFA's stated aim to provide scope for a greater share for developing countries in world trade in these products, with GATT data showing that this share has stagnated at between 25 and 26 per cent since 1977 and that in some developed countries the proportion of imports of textiles and clothing from developing countries has fallen. And thirdly, one can contrast the clause in the MFA which states that "restraints on exports from participating countries . . . . should normally be avoided if the exports from such countries represent a small percentage of the total imports of textiles covered by this Arrangement of the importing country concerned", with quotas imposed by the EEC, Canada, Sweden, Norway and other countries on imports from developing countries, usually the poorer ones, which supply well under one per cent of the total for the product concerned.

3.66   On the other hand, it is not easy to explain how such controls have been developed under an Arrangement whose "basic objectives shall be to achieve the expansion of trade, the reduction of barriers to such trade and the progressive liberalisation of world trade in textile products . . . ." and in which it is stipulated that "actions taken under this Arrangement should . . . . provide increased access to their markets for textile products from developing countries". It is perhaps even more difficult to explain how as recently as last December, in the conclusions adopted by the GATT Textiles Committee, the first of these two objectives was reiterated, although admittedly there was no mention of the second.

3.67   What is required as a start in the textiles/clothing sector is a return to multilateralism, and for the often relatively unexceptionable provisions of the MFA to be the ones which really determine market access, rather than simply providing a framework for highly protectionist bilateral agreements imposed by powerful importing countries on less powerful and often weak exporting countries. For this to occur it is necessary that the MFA should be brought within the rules and procedures of an improved Article XIX on the lines set out in paragraph 3.55 above and elaborated in Chapter 7. Within the context of such improved safeguard provisions, developed countries should undertake a phased liberalisation of imports of textiles and clothing from developing countries. This would require, in the early stages, that developed countries increase the annual growth in quotas and eliminate them altogether for small suppliers and new entrants (as enjoined by the MFA); they should then abolish all quotas on these products (even if this meant a strictly time-bound increase in tariffs); finally, within a specified time-bound period, they should reduce their m.f.n. duties to a level much nearer the average for all manufactures.

Footwear
3.68   Footwear and other segments of leather manufacturing usually employ labour-intensive methods of production and are thus generally considered 'sensitive' from a trade point of view. Tariffs are therefore high (averaging 13.2 per cent on an import-weighted basis for footwear and travel goods in the major developed countries[21]) and were not normally reduced under the Tokyo Round. Moreover, GSP concessions are minimal.

3.69   Reflecting a sharp increase in imports and in market penetration, NTMs on footwear have been applied by most major developed countries: the EEC has negotiated VERs with Rep. of Korea and Taiwan under which it regulates imports of non-leather footwear into certain member states; the United States has operated OMAs on footwear from the same two countries, although these expired in mid-1981 and were extended only in

56

the case of Taiwan (excluding athletic footwear); Canada has imposed quotas on footwear since 1977 under GATT Article XIX; Australia has a quota-determined licensing system for most types of footwear; Japan operates strict quotas in addition to its high tariffs. Generally, however, the coverage and intensity of the restrictions is far less than for textiles and clothing, and though the European Federation of Footwear Manufacturers has continued to seek an MFA type of arrangement, increased protection is being resisted.

3.71   The United States negotiated OMAs for colour television sets with Rep. of Korea and Taiwan for seventeen months from the beginning of 1979 and renewed them for two years from July 1980, although the combined quota of the two countries was increased by 36 per cent. The US tariff on citizens' band radios, raised from 6 to 21 per cent in 1978 as a safeguard, was progressively reduced to 15 per cent in 1980 and reverted to its original level in 1981. In the EEC, television and radio sets and parts have not been liberalised and are still liable to quantitative national restrictions. On imports of black and white televisions, for example, France and Italy have maintained quotas while those instituted by the United Kingdom on Rep. of Korea and Taiwan in 1977 under Article XIX of the GATT have since been converted into VERs. Imports of audio equipment have also been affected by NTMs (principally VERs) and those of colour televisions from developing countries are likely to be drawn into the net once the current patent licences lose their protective effect.[22] Efforts by EEC manufacturers to regulate imports at a Community level are continuing; some products (e.g. colour televisions from Japan) have been placed under statistical surveillance and an anti-dumping investigation has been undertaken on imports of black and white televisions from Rep. of Korea. All this is in addition to relatively high tariffs (14 per cent on radio and television sets, for example) which were not reduced under the Tokyo Round; moreover, because these products are treated as 'sensitive', they have been granted few concessions under the GSP. Television and radio components, too, are deemed 'sensitive' (as are calculators) and some are accorded tariff quotas and quantitative restrictions.

Electrical and Electronics Goods
3.70   Exports of a wide range of electrical and electronics components and finished products have constituted one of the most buoyant sources of foreign exchange for some developing countries in recent years. Based on labour-intensive assembly processes in low cost locations and using relatively mature and stable technologies available under licence from transnational corporations, the industry has 'internationalised' itself under sub-contracting and other intra-firm arrangements to such an extent that widespread protectionist pressures have been resisted despite the rapid

growth of developed country imports from developing countries. Certain problems have nevertheless arisen and some degree of 'new' protection by means of NTMs has occurred.

3.71   The United States negotiated OMAs for colour television sets with Rep. of Korea and Taiwan for seventeen months from the beginning of 1979 and renewed them for two years from July 1980, although the combined quota of the two countries was increased by 36 per cent. The US tariff on citizens' band radios, raised from 6 to 21 per cent in 1978 as a safeguard, was progressively reduced to 15 per cent in 1980 and reverted to its original level in 1981. In the EEC, television and radio sets and parts have not been liberalised and are still liable to quantitative national restrictions. On imports of black and white televisions, for example, France and Italy have maintained quotas while those instituted by the United Kingdom on Rep. of Korea and Taiwan in 1977 under Article XIX of the GATT have since been converted into VERs. Imports of audio equipment have also been affected by NTMs (principally VERs) and those of colour televisions from developing countries are likely to be drawn into the net once the current patent licences lose their protective effect.[22] Efforts by EEC manufacturers to regulate imports at a Community level are continuing; some products (e.g. colour televisions from Japan) have been placed under statistical surveillance and an anti-dumping investigation has been undertaken on imports of black and white televisions from Rep. of Korea. All this is in addition to relatively high tariffs (14 per cent on radio and television sets, for example) which were not reduced under the Tokyo Round; moreover, because these products are treated as 'sensitive', they have been granted few concessions under theGSP. Television and radio components, too, are deemed 'sensitive' (as are calculators) and some are accorded tariff quotas and quantitative restrictions.

Metal Products
3.72   Among the large number of simple metal products entering international trade, protectionism has so far affected only a few items of importance to developing countries. Tariffs on cutlery are well above average (17-19 per cent in the EEC and approaching 80 per cent for some items in the United States, for instance) and were usually exempted from cuts under the Tokyo Round, although the industry never acquired fully 'sensitive' treatment under the GSP. In addition VERs are operated on an unofficial industry-to-industry basis by several importing countries, including the United Kingdom, Germany (F.R.), Denmark, Norway and the Benelux countries, with various exporting countries, notably Rep. of Korea. In practice, however, these have not restricted trade to any great extent.   Another item of importance has been industrial fasteners (nuts, bolts, etc), where Indian and Korean exports to the United States were the subject of countervailing duty action in 1980.

58

Steel

3.73 The continued growth in steel-making capacity and decline in developed countries' demand after 1974, combined with an increase in capacity in certain newly industrialising countries (NICs) and centrally planned economies, have created substantial excess capacity and weak markets. In an effort to overcome these problems both the United States and EEC have instituted restructuring programmes whose external elements have involved a number of NTMs. However, the current situation remains serious in both markets and new trading conflicts have recently developed between their steel producers.

3.74 In the United States the 'trigger price mechanism' introduced in February 1978 to expedite investigations into subsidised or dumped imports has been suspended twice as a result of independently filed anti-dumping actions by domestic steel producers. Under the mechanism, which covered most carbon steel products, imports at prices below periodically adjusted floor levels based on the production costs of the most efficient steel manufacturer (deemed to be Japan) automatically led to anti-dumping investigations unless granted pre-clearance.[23] The mechanism was suspended in March 1980 and renewed in October of that year, strengthened by the introduction of an anti-surge provision which operated when domestic capacity utilisation fell below 87 per cent and which could lead to the imposition of anti-dumping or countervailing duties. A similar mechanism was instituted for special (alloy) steels, whereby anti-dumping investigations were conducted if import penetration exceeded the average for the previous ten years.

3.75 Although these measures had some effect on the NICs, particularly Brazil and Rep. of Korea, they were used mainly against other developed countries, especially the EEC. It was as a result of a barrage of anti-subsidy and anti-dumping petitions from the major US steel producers against imports from the EEC that the mechanism was suspended again in January 1982. After negotiations between the parties had broken down on the issue of market shares, the US Department of Commerce in June imposed countervailing duties against steel from seven European countries, Brazil and South Africa. The calculation of the subsidies, which has led to duties ranging from 0.5 to over 40 per cent of the price of the imported steel, is being disputed by the EEC.

3.76 In the EEC all intra- and extra-Community trade in iron and steel is now regulated, and about three-quarters of production is also controlled by quotas, which were recently extended to June 1983. As part of the Davignon Plan for reconstructing the industry, VERs were concluded with more than a dozen exporting countries[24] and provide for 'quantitative targets' (bilateral quotas) based on 'traditional trade flows' and consistent with the maintenance of stable domestic prices. In consonance with domestic market conditions, quotas in 1981 were set at around an eighth below imports in 1980, and though there has been some increase in 1982, no carry-over is being allowed and the total remains below the 1980 out-turn. For those imports not covered by bilateral agreements, provisional anti-dumping duties may be applied whenever delivered prices are below the Community's basic prices (set in relation to the costs of production in the most efficient producer, usually deemed to be Japan).

Wood Products
3.77   There is quite substantial protection of this sector by a number of developed countries. Plywood and veneers, for example, are considered 'sensitive' by several members of the EEC and where the GSP is applied it has quota limitations; other developed countries also protect this industry (Australian imports of thick plywood are under quota, for instance). The main developing countries affected are Rep. of Korea, Taiwan, Malaysia, Philippines and Brazil. The last of these has also faced access problems in the case of its rapidly expanding exports of pulpwood for the manufacture of paper — itself a highly 'sensitive' item.

Other Sectors
3.78   Protectionism exists in various other manufacturing sectors, but in general it has not yet had a particularly significant impact on developing country exports. In motor vehicles, for example, VERs have been instituted by several developed countries, but so far they have been directed at other developed countries, almost entirely Japan. So long as developing country car and component exports are 'regulated' by transnational corporations' intra-industry or intra-firm reciprocal trade arrangements, direct forms of protection may be unlikely, but when 'national' companies start to export 'indigenous' vehicles in large numbers the situations could alter.

3.79   Another sector where most of the friction in trade so far has occurred between developed countries is chemicals, where quotas have been applied by the EEC on certain petrochemicals from the United States. Difficulties may arise between developed and developing countries in the future, however, possibly quite soon between, say, Taiwan or Rep. of Korea and Japan, and later between OPEC and developed countries in general.

3.80   Shipbuilding is a rather different case, in that protectionism by developed countries takes the form not of border-controls but of subsidies by way of low cost export credits, tax exemptions, government

60

procurement policies, etc. Although subsidies have on occasions been high, the degree of protection thus afforded has in general been reasonably moderate, and several developing countries, notably Rep. of Korea, Brazil and Taiwan, have increased their share of the world market considerably.

3.81 Finally, developed country tariffs have been relatively high on imports of products from a number of miscellaneous light manufacturing industries in which developing countries have gained a comparative advantage, principally toys and sports goods, but also including a whole range of personal items like smoking pipes, musical instruments and umbrellas. However, these duties do not seem to have had much dampening effect on exports and market penetration; moreover, the items are not usually considered 'sensitive' and thus NTMs, although not unheard of, are rare.[25] Being manufactured by relatively insignificant industries in developed countries, the products concerned seem unlikely to face substantial barriers in future.

Overall Position

3.82 From the above brief survey it is possible to reach a number of conclusions. Chief among these is that many of the new protectionist measures against manufactures have discriminated against developing countries. For not only has it been on the products in which these countries are primarily interested that most of the new quantitative restrictions have been imposed, but it is also the developing countries (especially the poorer ones) which have suffered most from the increase in disputes resulting from the imprecise nature of the GATT codes and other instruments (including technical standards). The most important restrictions, as far as developing countries are concerned, have been on textiles and clothing; exports of this group of products are so significant for these countries, and increasingly so for the poorer and smaller ones, that they regard developments under the umbrella of the MFA as a barometer of developed country attitudes towards protectionism in general. Their experience in this respect has been discouraging, particularly since 1977. Worrying signs of strengthening protectionist pressures also exist in certain other sectors, notably steel and motor vehicles, which though not yet of widespread import to developing countries have important implications for their development prospects.

3.83 On the other hand, in certain other sectors again, such as footwear and possibly consumer electrical and electronics goods, protectionism does not appear to have gathered pace significantly in recent years. There are in addition many manufactures, notably in various branches of the engineering sector, in which developed country tariff protection is relatively low, NTMs virtually non-existent[26], and where spontaneous market adjustment has allowed developing countries to take full opportunity of their comparative advantage to develop exports in a most promising manner. It is in these areas at least as much as in the more traditional products that developing countries need to direct their future efforts at earning the foreign exchange necessary to implement their vital development plans and programmes. Such efforts will only bear fruit, however, if liberal market access continues to be granted to the products concerned. The recent experience in some manufacturing sectors casts doubts on the degree of confidence which can be placed on such an assumption.

IV – Services

3.84   Much of the discussion on international trade policy has been concerned with tangible goods. In contrast, international trade in services has received little attention. Although the contribution of services to domestic product and employment in individual countries is usually related to income levels and the degree of sophistication and maturity of the economy, the importance of the sector has increased considerably for almost all countries, developed and developing. According to one estimate, services accounted in 1978 for at least the same proportion of the GDP of the GATT contracting parties, in aggregate, as did the manufacturing sector. Moreover, technological advances in certain services, particularly in transport and communications, and the growing integration of the world economy, have led to a greater inter-nationalisation of service industries. For developing countries, service exports on a broad definition are now about one-third of merchandise exports, a higher proportion than for the world as a whole. With its increased importance and the participation of a large number of countries in international trade in services, it seems desirable that greater attention should be given to the development of a multilateral framework and international rules for trade in this sector.

3.85   Most of the services that are traded internationally are, in fact, closely linked to international trade in goods, though some (e.g. health and entertainment) are in the nature of 'consumption' services; others which also constitute a distinct category include 'factor' services (e.g. returns on capital and labour). Preliminary surveys suggest that services linked with international trade in goods are subject to the same types of restraint (subsidies; regulatory practices, particularly affecting rights of estab-lishment and market access; government procurement procedures; technical standards; licences, etc.) as those that impede the trade in goods, though not all of them are applied to each service industry. Other restrictions that are more specifically related to services, can still be regarded as non-tariff barriers and treated in a similar manner.

3.86   However, there are a number of special features of trade in services which have prevented progress towards liberalisation similar to that achieved for internationally traded goods. To begin with, there are serious problems in identifying, cataloguing and measuring the NTMs that exist in the services sector. There is also the problem of heterogeneity of different service industries, which makes it more difficult to establish generic and multilateral rules for the services sector as a whole. More fundamental, perhaps, are structural factors that determine the conditions under which different service activities are undertaken. For a variety of reasons, such as sovereignty, domestic policy and financial viability considerations, service industries, particularly banking, insurance and shipping, are subject in most countries, developed and developing, to a high degree of national regulation and state participation and, in some cases, to 'self-regulation' by professional bodies. Moreover, given the different levels of development and the contribution that services make to different economies, it is not always clear that removal of restrictions would be advantageous to all countries, particularly to developing countries and some of the smaller developed countries which are not in a position to become significant exporters of services in the foreseeable future.

3.87   It is therefore hardly surprising that past efforts to liberalise trade in services have been limited and not particularly successful. For example, GATT efforts in the 1950s to develop a set of rules regarding transport and insurance came to very little, largely because the developing countries could not support a recommendation for non-discrimination (i.e. no preference for domestic suppliers) and wanted to remain free to protect their domestic insurance industries. Even within the OECD, the Code of Liberalisation of Current Invisible Operations contains important reservations with regard to insurance. A number of governments have continued to insist that liberalisation of international transactions in this field must be preceded by a substantial degree of international harmonisation of national laws and regulations on insurance supervision and other legal and fiscal provisions. In the Tokyo Round, the question of restrictions on trade in services was not discussed in a systematic way. Apart from the inclusion of services where they are a part of a contract to supply goods, which is within the scope of the Procurement Code, little of significance was achieved for services in the MTNs.

3.88   Even now, it is possible to exaggerate the likely impact on future negotiations of the growing interest of some countries in the liberalisation of trade in services. For example, with the existing Federal and State laws on banks crossing interstate lines, it will hardly be possible for the United States to accept a strict application of the principle of reciprocity. In fact, it is far from clear that the US Government, at present the most active with

63

regard to international rules for trade in services, has decided on its objectives regarding the concepts, format or fora for any negotiations which might eventually take place in this field. More generally, different service industries are dealt with by different departments and regulatory agencies in all countries and governments seem to be administratively ill-prepared to conduct comprehensive multilateral negotiations in this sector.

3.89   While there seems to be, therefore, little immediate prospect of serious multilateral negotiations on services, substantial preparatory work will be useful in a number of areas. In the first place, there is a need for technical work in the GATT and UNCTAD secretariats and elsewhere to identify clearly the existing restrictions and trade practices in the various service industries so that different groups of countries will be better placed to recognise their specific interests. Secondly, countries need to clarify the policy alternatives available to them and make appropriate choices in the light of their economic objectives and circumstances. In this context, the varying roles that governments play in service industries, and the possibility of reconciling the interests of countries with surpluses in invisible balances and of those, usually developing countries, with deficits, would require careful assessment. Thirdly, before any multilateral negotiations could make significant progress, several operational issues would need to be considered extensively. They include the role of a comprehensive and multilateral framework, limitations of existing GATT and OECD Codes, the need for sector-specific arrangements, the format of negotiations, the possibilities of developing acceptable packages of gains and concessions, and the respective roles of the various international agencies concerned. Given these requirements for any eventual negotiations, a comprehensive programme of studies and analyses is required to assist governments to make an informed assessment of the extent and form of the existing restraints on service industries and to define the possibilities for improvement. A co-ordinated effort between GATT, UNCTAD and other international agencies would be desirable for this purpose.

References

1. Odd Gulbransen and Assar Lindbeck, *The Economics of the Agricultural Sector,* The Industrial Institute for Economic and Social Research, Stockholm, 1973.

2. E.A. Saxon and K. Anderson, "Japanese Agricultural Protection in Historical Perspective", *Australia-Japan Research Centre,* Canberra, May 1982.

3. FAO, *Commodity Review and Outlook, 1979-80,* p.112.

4. OECD, *Study on Problems of Agricultural Trade,* May 1982, para 5.19.

5. There is no widely recognised definition of processed products; the term is used in this chapter broadly to cover the end-products of any activity where the primary product represents the major material input into the product transformation operation.

6. This was shown in a recent study by UNCTAD. See UNCTAD, *The Processing Before Export of Primary Commodities: Areas for Further International Co-operation,* May 1979.

7. See forthcoming joint Commonwealth Secretariat/World Bank studies on *Industrial Processing of Primary Products* (J. McNerney, "Coconut oil refining"; R.C. Wanigatunga, "Processing of natural rubber of South Asian countries for the export market"; and J. Karunasekera, "The industrial processing of cocoa").

8. UNCTAD, *The Processing Before Export of Primary Commodities, op. cit.,* pp.23-27.

9. UNIDO, *Mineral Processing in Developing Countries,* 1980, p.3.

10. Austria, Canada, EEC, Finland, Japan, Norway, Sweden, Switzerland and United States.

11. Defined as those products exported by, or in the multilateral trade negotiations request lists of, beneficiary countries of the Generalized System of Preferences.

12. S.A.B. Page, "The Revival of Protectionism and its Consequences for Europe", *Journal of Common Market Studies,* September 1981.

13. By contrast the proportion of imports of manufactures controlled by official safeguard action under GATT Article XIX changed little and, outside the MFA, remained small, 2 per cent in the EEC and USA for example. (See L.M. Gard and J. Riedel, "Safeguard Protection of Industry in Developed Countries: Assessment of the Implications for Developing Countries", *Weltwirtschaftliches Archiv.,* Band 116, Heft. 3, 1980.)

14. See D.B. Keesing and M. Wolf, *Textile Quotas Against Developing Countries,* Trade Policy Research Centre, 1980, who cite estimates of premia reaching around 15-25 per cent of the export value, depending on the state of supply and demand.

15. By January 1987 the average (import-weighted) m.f.n. duty into the major developed countries will decline by 22 per cent, to 8.8 per cent for textile yarns and fabrics, and by 18 per cent, to 16.8 per cent, for clothing.

16. Taiwan is not a signatory of the MFA, and EEC quotas on its products are imposed unilaterally.

17. Australian Industries Assistance Commission, *Annual Report 1980/81*.

18. It should be added that such arrangements provide for 'equitable and quantifiable' compensation to the exporting participant.

19. The 41 signatories to MFA II (EEC counted as one) accounted for over four-fifths of world trade in textiles and clothing. By mid-June 1982 the protocol covering MFA III had 26 signatories representing 35 countries. (They included Brazil, Colombia, EEC, Egypt, Finland, Hong Kong, Hungary, India, Japan, Korea (Rep.), Malaysia, Mexico, Pakistan, Peru, Philippines, Poland, Romania, Singapore, Sri Lanka, Switzerland, Thailand, Uruguay and United States.)

20. Calculated from *The European Community's Textile Trade,* European Commission, April 1981 (Appendix C). It may be noted that imports from industrial countries (outside the EEC) rose at an average annual rate of 11.2 per cent.

21. Rates vary considerably, however; 27 per cent on leather footwear in Japan but only 8 per cent in the EEC, for example.

22. VERs have already been agreed with Japan.

23. Pre-clearance was granted if an exporter could establish that his price, although below the 'trigger' level, was at or above the 'fair-value' defined by the anti-dumping statute. It was granted to certain producers in Canada and Mexico, but is currently suspended.

24. In 1980 these comprised Australia, Austria, Brazil, Bulgaria, Czechoslovakia, Finland, Hungary, Japan, Norway, Poland, Romania, Spain and Sweden; in 1981 Korea (Rep.) was added.

25. France has erected quotas against some items, e.g. toys and umbrellas from certain countries in eastern Asia.

26. Except in respect of technical standards, which are capable of use for protective purposes.

4. The Costs of Protection to Developing Countries

"Liberal access to OECD markets for the manufactured exports of developing countries is a fundamental condition for the successful evolution of the new patterns in the world economy".

Emile van Lennep, 1982

4.1   The emphasis in this chapter is on the effects on developing countries of barriers to their exports. Particular attention is given to the impact of different forms of protection, for even if levels of protection remain unaltered, there may be substantial benefits for exporters if the forms were to be changed. We concentrate on the barriers of the developed market-economy countries; less attention is given to the barriers erected by the developing countries themselves, even though they are on average higher than those of the developed countries. This relative neglect arises because the costs of such barriers tend to be borne by the countries imposing them. Many of these barriers may be unwise and may, in the longer run, have serious impact on the growth of the international economy. But there is little doubt that it is the barriers of the developed countries which most restrict international commerce and the growth of exports from the developing countries. In the following chapter attention is given to the costs of the barriers erected by developed countries to the countries which erect them.

4.2   The growth process varies among countries according to endowments of factors of production and national policies. For those countries with plentiful supplies of natural resources — mineral, forest, ocean or agricultural — the early stages of growth will tend to be concentrated in these areas. If the supplies of these resources are particularly abundant relative to population, and if export markets are available, high levels of income may be supported by industries dependent upon them — as, for example, in New Zealand and Australia. In other countries, less well endowed with such resources, the growth process will tend at an early stage to move into products and techniques of production well suited to low-cost labour, later shifting towards products and processes which use more capital and skilled labour. As growth proceeds the patterns and volumes of both imports and exports will alter. The erection by trading partners of barriers to either the exports or the imports of a country will restrict growth and lower real income below the levels that could otherwise have been achieved.

Exports and Growth

4.3   In the last thirty years, a number of developing countries have had considerable success by pursuing export-oriented policies. Japan, though no longer classified as 'developing', is a prime example. More frequently cited are the 'newly industrialising countries' or 'fast-growing exporters of manufactures' — particularly Taiwan, Hong Kong, Singapore and Rep. of Korea. Per capita annual growth rates of GDP of 7 per cent or more were achieved by Singapore, Rep. of Korea and Hong Kong over the sixties and seventies, rates that would have been quite impossible for such relatively small states in the absence of export markets.

4.4   For many countries in the nineteenth century, exports of primary products provided an 'engine of growth'. This growth was seen, contemporaneously and subsequently, to be greater than that attributable simply to the gains from producing according to static comparative advantage. In more recent years, labour-intensive manufactures appear to have served the same function for those newly industrialising countries which have followed export-oriented policies.

4.5   High and rising trade barriers inflict major harm on those countries which attempt to develop exports as the leading growth sector. Investments in export-oriented industries have their yields depleted and may collapse. As a consequence, difficulties are experienced in servicing debts incurred to finance development, including, sometimes, debts due to countries which have imposed the barriers. Development will be forced away from industries appropriate to the economy.

4.6   But it is not only the export-oriented 'engine of growth' products that may be stalled by the erection or threat of trade barriers (or by the stagnation of world trade). Many governments may choose a more inward-looking development strategy, even if it implies a lower growth of GDP. These more inward-looking and import-replacement development strategies also can be frustrated by the erection of trade barriers. Countries pursuing the import-replacement path typically restrain imports by a variety of tariff and non-tariff barriers and frequently maintain an overvalued rate of exchange. Those imports which are permitted are generally of the high-priority 'essential for development' nature and exports are the means by which these essential imports are financed. While the closing of export markets is not the only reason why countries pursuing import-replacement strategies have found it difficult to export — for the strategy itself implies internal discrimination against exports — the closure of markets can wreak havoc with development plans. The nature of the import-replacement strategy makes it difficult to switch from one export product to another, for the strategy is typically implemented within a system of controls which are inflexible except in the longer term. Thus export shortfalls have implied an inability to obtain essential inputs for key development projects which, in turn, has frustrated the growth of industries dependent upon these projects. Import-substitution strategies can, paradoxically, result in very high dependence on trade.[1]

4.7   In view of the variety of ways in which exports may contribute to growth, and the problems of identifying some of the channels, the task of calculating a total cost to the developing countries of the trade barriers in place is extremely difficult. Several economists have studied empirically the relation between the growth of exports and of real GNP. Covering a large number of developing countries and various periods from 1950 to 1975,[2] the studies found a strong link between export growth and overall growth rates, particularly for the more advanced countries. While some economists may have doubts regarding the direction of causation, few would doubt that restricting exports would inhibit growth. One estimate suggests that the increase in the GNP of Rep. of Korea and Taiwan would have been 37 and 25 per cent smaller, respectively, in 1973 if the rate of growth of their exports from 1966 to 1973 had been at the average level achieved by the ten developing countries in the sample, this despite the suggestion that the empirical technique tended to underestimate the relationship. On the other hand, the increase in the GNP of Chile, India and Mexico, respectively, would have been 14, 12 and 8 per cent greater if these countries had experienced export growth rates equal to the average in the sample.[3]

4.8   In this chapter, further calculations of this nature are not attempted. Rather, calculations that have been made of the trade restraining impact of existing barriers are reported. Consideration is then given to the differential impact of alternative forms of protection designed to achieve the same objectives. Particular attention is directed to identifying those aspects of the current barriers which, without adding significantly to the achievement of the objectives of the countries imposing them, have a specially deleterious effect on exporting countries.

The Impact of Protection on Exports

1. Manufactured Goods

4.9   While there have been some estimates of the impact on exports of trade restrictions on manufactures, these are rather dated and generally do not include the effects of the crucially important non-tariff measures. One study concludes that exports of manufactures by developing countries in 1974 could have been 16 per cent greater if tariffs had been reduced by 60 per cent (and textile import quotas relaxed sufficiently to allow these additional exports).[4] But as even the documentation of non-tariff measures affecting imports of manufactures is far from complete — and, by their very nature, it is doubtful whether the documentation will ever be exhaustive — it is not surprising that comprehensive calculations of the restraining effects of these barriers are not available. Calculations which do not include them must be treated as substantial underestimates of the total effects of protection.

4.10   One way of attempting to show the impact of the 'new protectionism' is to examine the extent to which the penetration of developed country markets by developing countries has been arrested. The developing countries' annual growth in market penetration of 14 major OECD countries (as measured by their share in the apparent consumption of manufactures in these countries) was about 13 per cent for the years 1970-74 but thereafter fell sharply, so that for the decade as a whole it averaged only 8 per cent per annum.[5] While this average growth for the 1970s was higher than the 5 per cent per annum of market penetration by all imports, the sharp fall in the second half of the decade reflects the protectionist bias against the developing countries, and this has not abated.

4.11   Textiles and clothing still constitute one of the largest components of developing countries' exports of manufactures, although their share is declining. The deterioration in the position for developing countries in these products can be illustrated, as in Table 4.1, by comparing the growth of developed countries' imports from other developed countries and from developing countries during the three periods 1963-73, 1973-76 and 1976-79. The change was particularly marked in the case of clothing, where growth in developed countries' imports from developing countries had been approaching double that from other developed countries in the first period. In the years 1973-76 the rate of growth of imports from developing countries held up rather well while imports from developed countries fell. In the last three years of the 1970s, however, the rate of growth of imports from developing countries was substantially below that from developed countries. Finally, in 1980 developed countries' exports of textiles and clothing each rose more quickly than did their imports (including intra-

70

trade in each case), and their net deficit with developing countries diminished.

TABLE 4.1
Real Growth Rates of Imports of Clothing and Textiles by Western Europe and North America[a]
(average annual percentage increases)

Imports from	Clothing			Textiles		
	1963-73	1973-76	1976-79	1963-73	1973-76	1976-79
Developing countries	21.1	14.4	4.6	6.9	-0.4	4.6
Southern Europe	28.8	6.4	8.4	13.8	-0.8	9.2
Developed countries	11.7	-0.4	7.3	7.8	-4.5	5.0
All countries [b]	15.3	5.6	6.5	8.0	-3.6	5.3

a Comprising imports by the EEC, European Free Trade Association (excluding Portugal), United States and Canada. Imports are deflated by the United Nations value index for developed country manufactured exports to developing countries.

b Including centrally-planned economies.

Source: G.Curzon *et al., MFA Forever?* Trade Policy Research Centre, October 1981.

4.12   It is significant that in both 1963-73 and 1976-79 the rate of growth of imports of textiles from Southern Europe was double that from the developing countries. Clothing imports from Southern Europe also grew more rapidly than from the developing countries.

4.13   A rough guide to the impact of recent events and actions on the exports of developing countries can be obtained by observing changes in the relation between the income of the developed countries and their imports from the developing countries. One estimate[6] is that clothing imports from the developing countries would have been around 90 per cent (some $10 billion) greater in 1980 than they were, if the income elasticity of demand in developed countries for imports of manufactures from developing countries had remained the same as between 1968 and 1976; the increase for textiles would have been around a quarter (about $1 ¼ billion). To some extent this loss in potential earnings was countered by increased exports of other manufactures, but it occurred, of course, in products in which the developing countries — and particularly the poorer countries — have a marked comparative advantage.

2. Primary Products

4.14   Studies of primary products are more common and complete, although there is a wide range of results. One estimate was made of the increased value of exports of 99 food products and their derivatives that would accrue to 56 developing countries if 18 major OECD countries reduced tariffs and non-tariff barriers by 50 per cent.[7] Overall it was estimated that these exports would increase by $3 billion per annum (in 1977 dollars, based on 1975-77 exports), which is 11 per cent of actual agricultural exports by these developing countries in the base years.[8]

4.15 Over four-fifths of these gains were estimated to accrue to developing countries in the middle-income bracket, though agricultural exports of low-income countries showed an increase of 8½ per cent. The largest increases in gross revenues would be registered by Brazil, Argentina, India, Philippines, Thailand and Colombia. Latin America would receive 60 per cent of the increase and Asia 23 per cent. On a net basis, the increase for India and for most other low-income countries would be much less, and in some cases (e.g. Bangladesh) could be negative (owing to higher world prices). It was also estimated that the real income gain for the 56 developing countries, taking into account the effects of the hypothetical OECD agricultural trade liberalisation on both imports and exports and the cost of producing the additional exports, would be about $500 million per annum (in 1977 dollars). Excluding wheat from the liberalisation programme would increase this real income gain significantly, as the developing countries are substantial net importers of this grain. However, for a number of reasons these results may underestimate the increases in the value of exports and in real income which would occur. For example, the full effect of tariff escalation in discriminating against processed products is probably not captured.

4.16 With regard to processed products it has been estimated that removing tariffs on imports of the processed forms of eight agricultural products, in which developing countries already have a significant share of world exports, would have increased the value added in developing country processing activities by 20 per cent or more and would have boosted export revenues by more than the GSP has done.[9]

4.17 Another study has attempted to capture some longer-term effects of agricultural protection by examining the changing composition of exports of primary food products to EEC countries between 1962 and 1979.[10] Thus, for example, whereas New Zealand provided 21 per cent of the EEC countries' imports of cheese and curd in 1962, that percentage had shrunk to zero in 1979. As a result of losses in market shares (mainly caused by the Community's Common Agricultural Policy (CAP) and reflected in increased intra-EEC trade), it is estimated that developing countries had lost exports to the EEC of $2.9 billion in 1979. (Other large losses were: Australia, $1.1 billion; New Zealand, $1.8 billion, and the United States, $0.7 billion.) This is a rough and ready calculation.[11] But again it is suggestive of an order of magnitude.

72

Forms of Protection

4.18   From the point of view of exporters, it would be most desirable if importers ceased protection. Many objectives of governments of importing countries may be better achieved by policies of assistance that are not linked to the continued production of particular goods.[12]

4.19   If assistance is tied to the production of particular goods, payment of production subsidies (bounties) is a means by which the harmful effects on exporters may be contained. Imports will be curtailed to the extent that production is sustained. On the other hand, as the prices paid by consumers are not raised by such a policy, demand is not restrained. With regard to stability of world prices, if prices for the protected producers are kept constant by production subsidies while world prices are oscillating, some instability is exported onto world markets, but not to the extent that occurs with some other protective devices.

4.20   It has been suggested[13] that in practice many such subsidies have been increased to an extent that would not have been possible with other forms of protection — due to lack of international scrutiny and to the ability of bureaucrats to 'tailor-make' regulations to satisfy various pressure groups. The supposed restrictiveness of budgetary considerations on such subsidies does not always apply, it is argued, particularly when the subsidies are given by tax exemptions rather than by direct payments. Nevertheless, while there may be particular exceptions the direct subsidy method generally has advantages over most other forms of protection.[14]

4.21   Calculations can be made of the expansion of trade which could occur if production subsidies replaced other forms of protection though in a way in which the actual level of protection is unchanged. In Table 4.2, such estimates are shown for Japan, Germany (F.R.), France and the United Kingdom, for several agricultural commodities. Beef is the commodity in which the most dramatic impact on trade could be expected to occur, particularly in Japan, with net imports for the four countries increasing eighteen-fold. Net imports of sugar, wheat and barley could be expected to increase about 70 per cent, while the relatively smaller increase in maize imports is in excess of a million tonnes. While much of the benefit of such increased imports would flow to developed country exporters, much would also be available to developing country exporters, particularly in South America and, for sugar, in some Commonwealth countries. Two points should be noted about these calculations: first, they assume no change in the level of protection for producers in the four countries, only in its form; and secondly, they are for 1976, and the disparity between world and internal prices in the EEC has increased significantly since then, implying that the proportionate increase in imports of EEC countries would now be much larger.

TABLE 4.2
Effect on Consumption and Trade of Replacing Existing
Forms of Protection by Production Subsidies[a]
1976

	France	Germany (F.R.)	U.K.	Japan	Total of four countries Increased consumption ('000 tonnes)	Increased net imports (%)
		Increased consumption ('000 tonnes)				
Wheat	321	476	219	147	1,163	69
Maize	424	548	325	-35	1,262	16
Barley	316	538	16	174	1,044	71
Sugar	122	180	143	72	517	70
Beef	254	297	120	932	1,603	1,781

a Bale and Lutz provide high and low estimates for elasticities; the figures shown here derive from simple averages of these two.

Source: Calculated from data in Malcolm D. Bale and Ernest Lutz, "Price Distortions in Agriculture and their Effects: An International Comparison", *American Journal of Agricultural Economics,* February, 1981, Tables 1 and 2.

4.22   Tariffs raise prices facing consumers as well as the prices received by producers, and both these impacts tend to reduce imports and depress world prices. As long as duties are at fixed rates, existing and potential exporters who reduce their export prices will be able to gain additional access. But this access does not exist when the trade barriers take the form of variable import levies which allow the maintenance of fixed internal prices that do not alter with world market conditions. Similarly, import quotas and so called 'voluntary export restraints' (VERs) give little opportunity for competitive entry by existing or potential exporters — they cartelise the trading system. This cartelisation may not be too harmful for some existing exporters, for they may be able to share in the gains from such restriction. This applies particularly in the cases of VERs and bilateral (rather than global) quotas. However, new entrants tend to be excluded. Exports can hardly be an engine of growth under such arrangements. Thus, the Multifibre Arrangement, by almost freezing quota allocations, has all but denied countries as varied as Sri Lanka, Bangladesh, Mauritius or Indonesia the chance of seriously fostering export-oriented manufacturing in this, the archetypal activity for a less industrially advanced developing country. At the same time, it has taken away from more industrially advanced developing countries, such as the Philippines, Pakistan or Colombia, the incentive to make the necessary policy adjustments to their textile and clothing industries.

4.23   Variable import levies and other trade barriers which allow constant internal prices to be maintained insulate the internal economy from world price variations. By refusing to share the effects of world instability, countries imposing such measures aggravate instability in the rest of the world. In this regard variable import levies, as under the EEC's CAP,are similar to the state trading policies of centrally planned economies and to other import controls under which the level of imports is determined by the aim of domestic stability. Such protective devices tend to aggravate instability in exporting countries (as well as in other importers) and from this point of view, as well as in their depressing effects on world prices, they are generally regarded as having harmful effects on exporters.

4.24   Instability has been of most importance in primary product markets and the EEC's CAP, together with the increasing insulation of the East European and Japanese markets, has been a major force in exporting instability. It has been argued that the increased insulation of major importers from world market conditions caused world grain prices to fluctuate more widely in the early 1970s than a decade earlier, even though the disturbance — in terms of a shortfall in world grain production below trend — was substantially smaller.[15] It might be noted, however, that it is not only the developed countries which attempt to insulate their food markets from instability. Developing countries do also, though typically for the benefit of consumers rather than producers.

4.25   As described in Chapter 3, the EEC's CAP is now even encouraging the building up of huge exportable surpluses of some products, which further disturb export markets of other countries, including developing countries. These surpluses do not appear to be the conscious aim of policy but rather are the by-product of the pursuit of the domestic objectives of income support and stability. The surpluses indicate clearly the inappropriate policies being used to achieve these objectives. Failing a substantial change in the form of policy weapon, acreage or production limitations would at least contain some of the most deleterious effects on traditional exporters.

4.26   Production subsidies, tariffs, import quotas and even variable import levies are generally imposed and implemented in a manner that is visible to existing and potential exporters. However, health, sanitary and 'standards' regulations, often applied in an arbitrary manner not intended by the legislature, increase uncertainty among existing exporters, are concealed from consumers and legislators, and leave hopeful potential exporters frustrated and often ignorant of the real source of their frustration. Lack of information creates uncertainty and requires the use of scarce resources to overcome it. Again, where market access can only be obtained as a result of extensive negotition, skilled officials are needed for the negotiations, and they are in short supply. These are real costs for exporters and are part of the protective barriers.

Centrally Planned Economies

4.27   So far in this chapter, attention has been directed at the effects on developing countries' exports of protective measures taken by developed countries with market economies. Since the majority of developing country exports are destined for these countries, their policies are of prime importance. But although exports to developed centrally planned economies constitute only a small proportion of the total (4 per cent in 1980 and 6 per cent of those from 'non-oil' developing countries), the effects of import restrictions by these countries are by no means insignificant. Several East European countries levy tariffs in much the same way as the developed market economies, but much more important are their policies of state procurement and bilateral balancing of trade which have effects similar to the more harmful forms of trade restraint imposed by the market economies. The relatively slow growth of developing countries' exports to the centrally planned countries is indicative of the degree of protection encountered. Although imports of food have been relatively buoyant since 1973, and those of steel, chemicals and machinery have risen quite swiftly (albeit from a very low base), growth in the important textiles and clothing sector has been sluggish even in terms of current values, and in volume the total was almost certainly lower in 1980 than it had been in 1973. Losses in potential export earnings in that sector at least must therefore have been very considerable if unquantified. It is important that markets in the centrally planned economies should be made more open to trade with the developing countries.

Developing Countries

4.28   To complete the picture, reference should also be made to the losses to individual developing countries' potential exports caused by protection in other developing countries. No aggregate estimates are available of these losses, but an indication of their size may be gained by reference to two statistics: first, intra-trade among developing countries in 1980 was 26 per cent of their total trade (22 per cent if trade with the major oil exporters is excluded); and secondly, the average tariff levied by those developing countries for which that information is available was 46 per cent, ranging from 11 per cent for metallic ores to 91 per cent for beverages, tobacco and clothing.[16] Whilst it could no more be expected that all developing countries would abolish their protective barriers to imports than that all developed countries would do so, it would seem not unreasonable to expect the newly industrialising and other economically more advanced developing countries to reduce barriers considerably in the near future.

76

The boost to trade from such a move could be substantial, particularly in capital goods and equipment and semi-manufactures among the newly industrialising countries.

Overall Effects

4.29   It is of particular concern that countries are increasingly introducing forms of protection which have especially damaging effects. Having achieved significant reductions in tariffs — a relatively less costly form of protection — it is ironic that less transparent and more obnoxious forms are now developing. We recommend that particular attention be given to the aims of those imposing trade barriers and to the way in which these aims can be achieved with the least cost, particularly in so far as exporting countries are concerned.

4.30   Any country maintaining protective barriers or imposing new barriers that are inconsistent with its obligations under agreed international rules and procedures should have to justify its action in an open multilateral forum. Countries wishing to impose such protective barriers should be required to specify the economic aims of such barriers not only in terms of a trade objective but also in terms of underlying considerations such as maintenance of employment. The specification of such objectives would allow an opportunity for discussion of alternative ways of achieving the objectives, at less cost to exporters.

4.31   The really insidious damage done by protectionism is the long-term effects it has on government policies aimed at efficient economic development and on the attitudes of productive enterprises which would have to put such policies into operation. As the World Bank has stated, "the worst result of the increased protectionism may be a greater unwillingness on the part of many developing countries to risk more outward-looking trade policies, even where these are urgently needed. They could, therefore, suffer the consequences of inflexibility and low import capacity usually associated with inward-looking trade regimes — costs that are likely to be particularly high in an uncertain and protectionist international environment, where flexibility is at a premium. . . . the adverse effects of heightened protection may be felt more by the poorer and less successful developing countries than by the most successful and visible targets".[17] And, as noted above, even inward-looking trade regimes are also severely harmed by this protectionism.

References

1. A.O. Krueger, *Trade and Employment in Developing Countries,* forthcoming, Vol.3, "Synthesis and Conclusions", Ch.3.

2. See A.O. Krueger, *op.cit.,* for a summary of several of the studies.

3. B. Balassa, "Exports and Economic Growth: Further Evidence", *Journal of Development Economics,* Vol.5, 1978, pp.186-8. The other five countries were Argentina, Brazil, Colombia, Israel and Yugoslavia.

4. T.B. Birnberg, "Trade Reform Options: Economic Effects on Developing and Developed Countries", in W.R. Cline (ed.), *Policy Alternatives for a New International Economic Order: An Economic Analysis,* 1979.

5. H. Hughes and J. Waelbroeck, "Can Developing Country Exports Keep Growing?", *The World Economy,* 1981, pp.127-147.

6. UNCTAD Secretariat (unpulished), 1982.

7. A. Valdes and J. Zietz, *Agricultural Protection in OECD: its Costs to Less-developed Countries,* International Food Policy Research Institute, Dec. 1980.

8. The largest increases would accrue to sugar ($1.1 billion or a 29 per cent increase), vegetable oils, seeds and cake ($378 million or 7 per cent), meat (almost entirely beef — $336 million or 44 per cent), and coffee ($277 million or 4 per cent). Making allowance for exports from Cuba and from those developing countries whose 1975 populations were under 4 million, which were excluded from the developing countries selected, would raise the total increase considerably, probably to more than $4 billion.

9. World Bank, *World Development Report 1981,* p.23.

10. A.J. Yeats, "Contemporary Agricultural Protectionism: an analysis of international economic effects and options for institutional reform", 1982, mimeo.

11. It ignores gains that these exporters may have made from exports to third markets as a result of increased exporting from one EEC member to another; on the other hand it ignores the reduced imports of each EEC member arising from increased protection for its own farmers.

12. See also paras 3.23 and 5.4.

13. H. Hughes and J. Waelbroeck, *op. cit.*

14. It is, however, more difficult to incorporate preferential schemes into this system of protection than into some other forms.

15. D. Gale Johnson, "World Agriculture, Commodity Policy and Price Variability", *American Journal of Agricultural Economics,* 1975, p.826.

16. UNCTAD, *Protectionism and Structural Adjustment in the World Economy* (TD/B/888), 15 Jan. 1982.

17. World Bank, *World Development Report 1979,* p.22.

5. The Costs of Protection to Developed Countries

"It is depressing to think of all the effort wasted over generations, and the income foregone, because of the belief that an economy can gain by protecting its industries".

Jan Tumlir, 1982

5.1 All forms of protection, from a published tariff to an open or concealed subsidy, a quota on imports and other impediments to competition from abroad, involve intervention by government in order to assist particular domestic activities by placing foreign competitors under a handicap. The intention is usually to ensure the maintenance or enlargment of the resources engaged in the protected activity, either on a continuing footing or by giving time for a change of employment to some more remunerative activity. Sometimes there is a broader objective and the intention is not to favour any particular activity, but to achieve some radical transformation of the economy under close government control or to allow fuller employment of all available resources when international influences are exerting contractionary pressure.

5.2 Some forms of protection are explicitly designed to continue indefinitely. This applies particularly to the use of tariffs and to activities protected wholly or mainly on non-economic grounds. Often, however, the intention is that protection will last for a limited time while an adjustment is made to new economic circumstances. The justification of protection then becomes merged in the general case for economic management, with no clear line between intervention to control and re-direct domestic market forces and intervention to override the force of competition from foreign suppliers. The case against protection, at the same time, reduces either to the familiar argument that market forces are best left to operate freely without government intervention or, alternatively, that there are more effective or cheaper ways than protection to accomplish structural adjustment.

5.3   The arguments on both sides are clear whether one looks at protection to a single industry or at more comprehensive proposals to restrict imports. Governments priding themselves on their ability to pick 'winners' may offer support to a new industry that would have difficulty in establishing itself, whether in the face of foreign competition or for other reasons. The question is then whether governments are likely to assess correctly the prospect of ultimate viability. Their assessment, however, is likely to be on a different basis from that of private decision-takers in their weighing of the benefits expected as well as in the use made of available information, the assessment of risks and attention to them, and the willingness to take the long view. Similarly, governments may seek to help an existing industry that is in difficulties and make use of import restrictions for this purpose. While such help may allow the industry an opportunity for reconstruction, there must be some doubt whether the industry would take advantage of the opportunity and whether structural adjustment would not better take the form of grants for re-training, re-location, diversification, and so on. In both kinds of situation, moreover, the government has the option of restricting imports or offering a subsidy.

5.4   Where the object of protection is to raise or preserve the incomes of those who are engaged in the protected activities, this can be achieved with less harmful effects on other countries, as has often been argued (e.g. in GATT, UNCTAD and OECD[1]) by giving direct income supplements (and/or adjustment assistance) instead of tying the assistance to the output of some particular product. The assistance should be given to individuals and enterprises in forms that encourage the movement of resources out of activities in developed countries that are more suited to developing countries and not in ways that make for their retention in those activities. There is a constant need for structural adjustment in every economy, quite independently of competition from abroad, and it would help to minimise the transitional costs of such adjustments if governments were to formulate and give effect to policies and mechanisms encouraging greater mobility of resources.

5.5   More comprehensive measures of protection are usually proposed when there are difficulties in using the main instruments of economic management: monetary and fiscal policy and changes in the exchange rate. A rapidly increasing volume of imports or a mounting external deficit may threaten the maintenance of full employment (or indeed, in current circumstances, a recovery in the level of employment) and provoke agitation for the imposition of trade barriers across-the-board. Protection is not, however, a satisfactory means of regulating the level of employment and it would be unfortunate if the first thought of governments faced with rising unemployment was to put obstacles in the way of imports. The normal way of responding to pressure on the balance of payments is through the exchange rate, and it is only if for good reasons this cannot be allowed to fall that there can be any grounds for contemplating general limitations on the volume of imports.

5.6 Whatever the object of protection, the benefits offered to the interests protected have to be set against the costs to other domestic interests, and these have to be compared with the costs of alternative means of achieving the same objectives. We turn next to examine these costs.

Costs to Producers
5.7 In the short-term, protection is paid for by consumers in the form of higher prices and a reduced variety of goods. If it involves domestic subsidies there is also a cost to the taxpayer. In the longer period, there is a cost to producers as a group (whether workers, employers or shareholders) who, as exporters, risk losing sales through retaliatory action or, more directly, through the loss of purchasing power over imports in the countries affected. A cost may also be payable by the producer who is given protection, in as much as he is locked into an activity in which his productivity is likely to be lower than it could have been in another activity; in any case, he may eventually succumb to the competition from abroad and be put out of business. Again, this applies just as much to the worker in the protected activity as to his employer. Finally, there may be a cost to the whole community if the economy is not being operated as efficiently as would be possible without protection.

5.8 These costs may well exceed the benefits conferred on the groups enjoying protection. As with all government intervention favouring some particular activity or in furtherance of some proclaimed objective, the benefits are usually more immediately obvious, but the costs are just as real and need to be carefully assessed. That they are frequently overlooked is apparent from the way in which, in trade negotiations, it is almost invariably assumed that a country withdrawing any form of restriction or barrier is making a concession to the interests of citizens of other countries, not to its own, and is therefore entitled to demand reciprocal concessions from its trading partners.

5.9 The persistence and pervasiveness of protection do not result from a careful comparison of costs and benefits. They are usually caused by the exercise of political pressure by powerful groups of import-competing producers and workers. In the highly imperfect market in which policy-makers operate, producers and workers are relatively concentrated, vocal and well-organised, while consumers are more diffuse, quiescent and unorganised. Thus, even if the loss to consumers because of protection

81

exceeds the gain to producers, the large number of consumers over whom such losses are spread and the difficulty and cost of organising them militate against effective lobbying. Moreover, while the immediate costs of import penetration (resulting in, say, reduced profits or increased unemployment) are highly visible and capable of apparent quantification, the long-term benefits for consumers and producers alike (in the form of lower prices, greater variety, higher-paid jobs and faster economic growth) are much less visible and less easily assessed.

5.10 Differences between industries in the level of protection depend on the strength of common purpose in the industry, on its ability to organise and obtain the necessary resources to lobby for support, and on which industries are seen by the public as most 'deserving' on equity or other grounds. Protection is most likely in large, specialised, declining industries employing relatively immobile factors (especially labour) in a small area of a weak economy, where import penetration is severe but immediate prospects of alternative employment of labour or capital are poor and where foreign linkages are few if any. Thus, apart from the special case of agriculture, it is in industries such as textiles, clothing, footwear, steel and shipbuilding that pressures for protection are greatest and most frequently granted, rather than in industries producing, say, electrical goods and chemicals, in which demand is more buoyant, skills more transferable and the transnationals more active.

5.11 In the longer-term, however, the position looks rather different. The extent of intra-industry and inter-industry linkages in a modern economy is such that any artificially induced change in the supply-demand relationship in one segment has immediate repercussions in others. Protection is contagious: give it to one industry or enterprise and it is demanded by others, for in many parts of industry the output of one enterprise is the input of another.

5.12 The decline in the importance of tariffs and the strict conditions governing their use under the GATT have altered the political mechanism through which the level of protection is determined. The place of tariffs has been taken by a wide range of non-tariff measures which do not, as a rule, come before the legislature and are taken administratively. Such administered protection, although it differs from one country to another in the way in which discretion is exercised, involves extensive delegation to the bureaucracy and is inherently protectionist, since it is much easier to lobby for higher protection than to sue for reduced protection.

5.13 Unlike other government assistance to industry, protection may set off reactions abroad that counteract or destroy any benefits it is intended to bring. The foreigner does not usually ask whether protection is an appropriate response to some perceived divergence between market prices and social costs. He may grant that some forms of competition such as dumping are unfair and agree that they should be stopped by government action. But, for the most part, he sees nothing unfair in the prices he quotes and the competition he offers and regards all trade barriers as discriminating between him and domestic competitors. He is likely, therefore, to resent fresh barriers and urge remonstrance and retaliation on his government. Such retaliation, if it occurs, could go far to nullify any advantage to producers as a group although it might have comparatively little effect on the producers benefiting directly from protection. Similarly the repercussions of the exclusion of imports on the capacity of the countries affected to purchase goods abroad and on export markets elsewhere could be substantial. It is an illusion to suppose that if low-cost producers are denied access to the markets of developed countries, these countries can protect their industries from 'market disruption' without further inconvenience. We discuss this further below (paragraph 5.33).

Fair Labour Standards
5.14   Protection is sometimes demanded and justified by capital and labour in developed countries on grounds of 'unfair' competition by developing countries induced by low wages and 'unfair' labour standards. Workers in developed countries complain also that such 'unfair' labour practices aggravate unemployment by encouraging relocation of enterprises to developing countries. There have therefore been demands for the adoption of a 'social clause' in the GATT to assist in ensuring the adoption of minimum labour standards. Indeed this was proposed by the Commonwealth Trade Union Council in oral and written representations made to the Group. It was stressed by the Council that the 'social clause' was not meant to be some form of hidden protection. There is no doubt about the need to terminate inhumane labour conditions wherever they may still be practised. However, a distinction must be made between exploitation by particular employers of their bargaining power, resulting in the unfair treatment of the workers in their employment, and the relatively low pay and inferior conditions of work which reflect the economic circumstances of underdevelopment, low productivity and high unemployment and underemployment in developing countries. There is need for greater recognition of this distinction if the argument about 'unfair' labour standards is not to continue to be used to support and encourage protectionism. A 'social clause' in the GATT would be a concession to the argument and might help to confuse the issue further. It is not therefore considered necessary. The ILO has been concerned with establishing minimum labour standards. While such standards are necessary and are proving beneficial, they should always retain flexibility

to accommodate the vast differences in social and economic conditions between developed and developing countries.

Costs to Consumers
5.15 The consumer costs of protection are not easily quantified. Estimates which have been made of the effects on particular products point to a very large aggregate but the information for countries is sketchy.

5.16 One often quoted estimate[2] is that the protectionist measures imposed by the United States between 1975 and 1977 on goods imported from Asia and Latin America resulted in a loss to consumers of $1,250 million for carbon steel, $1,200 million for footwear, $660 million for sugar, $400 to $800 million for meat and $500 million for television sets, or over $4 billion on these five items. The consumer cost per job protected was more than $50,000 per year, at a time when American employment was growing at three million jobs every year despite import competition. Nevertheless, this subvention provided no guarantee of long-term job security. Another estimate,[3] also for the United States, put the costs of protection to consumers of clothing, footwear and sugar at $7.7 billion over a four year period.

5.17 In the United Kingdom the Consumers Association examined the costs for clothing and concluded that the Multifibre Arrangement (MFA), which covers the 60 per cent of British clothing imports from 'low-cost' countries, had increased prices by between 15 and 40 per cent and had created shortages, particularly of the lower-priced items. Most of the increase in prices was attributed to quota premia (retained by the suppliers) and the greatest effects were felt by the poorer consumers. Elsewhere in the EEC, a retail organisation found that, on average, the prices of textiles and clothing of comparable quality at the lower end of the price range were 30 to 40 per cent lower from ('low-cost') countries outside the EEC than those of similar goods made within it.[4] In Germany (F.R.) after 1976, when quota protection was tightened, the average price of apparel rose twice as fast as that of all manufactures, even though the country was probably the most liberal in the EEC in administering the MFA quotas.

5.18 Similar results have been found in other countries. In Canada, the annual cost to consumers of bilateral quotas on clothing instituted in 1979 has been estimated at C$198 million, while that of tariffs and quotas has been put at C$467 million.[5] It has been claimed that 6,000 man-years' employment have been created by this protectionist policy, but the annual cost to the Canadian consumer has amounted to approximately C$33,000 per job. Considering that the average annual wage in the clothing sector was less than C$10,000, the policy has been extremely costly; it has also been inefficient, the pure economic waste having been estimated at over C$14,000 per additional man-year of employment created.

5.19   In Australia, the total annual cost to consumers of protection in the clothing sector has been estimated at A$235 per household.[6] At the retail level it has been estimated that consumers pay A$1.1 billion more per year for clothing, drapery and footwear than they would if all assistance to the industries were withdrawn.

5.20   In the agricultural sphere protection is rife. While the European Community's Common Agricultural Policy (CAP) has been one of the most conspicuous examples, the same criticisms to which it has been subjected could have been made of the agricultural policy of almost any developed country. In almost all cases the prices paid by consumers are higher than necessary to ensure satisfactory supplies, while some of the human and capital resources retained within the sector could be redeployed elsewhere to produce goods of greater value to consumers. Agricultural support systems which raise the price of food are fiscally regressive and have an adverse effect on the distribution of real incomes.[7] As regards security of supply, even the European Commission has acknowledged that in the EEC this may have been achieved at a higher price than necessary.[8]

5.21   The amounts involved have been enormous. The annual cost to consumers and taxpayers of the CAP in the late sixties, when there were only six members, was put in two separate estimates at $14 billion or more. The cost of US farm programmes at that time was estimated at nearly $10 billion. For the world as a whole the cost of agricultural protection may have been in excess of $40 billion.[9]

5.22   More recent estimates put the cost to EEC consumers in 1978 of the three main items — wheat, sugar and dairy products — at $27 billion.[10] In Japan the extra costs for consumers of rice alone in the same year were estimated at over $10½ billion[11] while in the United States consumers of sugar and dairy products were paying nearly $4 billion in excess of world prices.[12]

5.23   But the costs of the CAP and other measures of protection involving subsidies to domestic producers are not felt only by consumers. They are also a considerable drain on taxpayers' resources, and it is to that aspect that we now turn.

Costs to Taxpayers
5.24   As various rounds of GATT multilateral trade negotiations have progressively diminished the possibilities of industrial protection through

the tariff, which is the one means of trade restraint whose direct effects are beneficial to the taxpayer, protectionism has depended increasingly on import quotas and production subsidies. The last of these has become a growing drain on the public purse and in most developed countries the revenue raised from tariffs is now but a fraction of the expenditure incurred in supporting industries in trouble.

5.25   Such troubles almost always take the form of over-capacity and a consequent under-utilisation of labour and capital resources. This may have been caused by an (unexpected) increase in import penetration but it may equally well have resulted from many other factors. These include changes in the level of economic activity and consumer income, changes in demand conditions including those caused by shifts in consumer taste or rapid technological developments, changes in conditions of supply of major inputs such as energy, consequential changes in relative prices, and the inevitable effects of sheer bad management and lack of reasonable foresight.

5.26   Major industries in whose protection the taxpayer has played an important role include steel, shipbuilding, textiles and motor vehicles, to which should of course be added the agricultural sector. In steel, a considerable amount of retrenchment has now occurred in the EEC, but there was a time during the second half of the 1970s when the cost of subsidies was phenomenal, not least in the United Kingdom.

5.27   In shipbuilding, government subventions by Germany (F.R.), the Netherlands and the United Kingdom totalled around $1.25 billion at the beginning of 1980. These are but three of the many industrial countries subsidising this activity, however, and a better indication of the relative burden incurred by the taxpayer is given by the estimate that for every job paying $20,000 a year in a Swedish shipyard, Swedish taxpayers have to pay an annual subsidy of from $40,000 to $50,000.[13]

5.28   In motor vehicles, the cost to the British taxpayer of subsidising BL cars has been substantial for some years, but it was not until the level approached $1 billion a year in the early 1980s that really significant adjustment measures were taken in the form of labour-shedding. Earlier, rather more positive use of taxpayers' funds had been made in Germany (F.R.) where after Volkswagen made a number of employees redundant as a result of sustaining losses of $300 million in 1974, the Government had set aside over $100 million to encourage new activities in the region affected. The measure was successful, the redundant workers cost the taxpayer under $3,500 each, and by 1975 Volkswagen was again profitable and recruiting.

5.29   Although most of the subsidies in the agricultural sector of developed countries are paid by the consumer, considerable amounts also fall on the taxpayer (although as far as individuals are concerned, the distinction between the two is somewhat academic except in so far as the burden on the consumer is fiscally regressive and that on the taxpayer tends to be progressive). In the EEC, the taxpayer has paid large sums to subsidise Community exports of agricultural products to third markets and to 'top-up' the producers' guaranteed price. Such subventions have reached some $2-3 billion in recent years and are still rising.

5.30   The costs of protection to taxpayers have been substantial: in 1976, for example, production subsidies alone are estimated to have reached 7 per cent of GDP in Norway and Ireland, 4 per cent in Belgium, and 3 per cent in France, Netherlands, Italy and the United Kingdom; revenues from tariff protection, by contrast, were put at under 3 per cent in each case.[14] But so often the subsidies have been used in an attempt to protect producers from structural change rather than to facilitate their adjustment to shifts in comparative advantage. Whilst such indiscriminately used funds can benefit producers in the short-term, their longer-run effects can be somewhat different, as the next section seeks to demonstrate.

Costs to the Economy
5.31   The costs of protection to a country's economy are more than the sum of the costs to its consumers, taxpayers and producers at a point in time. There are also long-term effects on the creation of employment, income and wealth through the limitation of the opportunities open to consumers and producers. Some of these arise from a misdirection of resources when competitive influences are held at bay, others from a weakened response to dynamic shifts in comparative advantage between and within enterprises, industries, regimes and countries. The cartelisation and muffling of competition which protection brings in its wake leads to structural rigidities and the freezing of production patterns; to the directing of productive resources to 'rent-seeking' activities; to the loss of incentives to reduce prices, improve products or respond to changes in consumer preferences; and to all the other manifestations of economic inefficiency which characterise sellers' markets.

5.32   It has been common in the past to minimise the costs of protection on the grounds that the foreigner will pay. But in any country forming only a small proportion of the world market, the chances of depressing the price at which imports are purchased are not very high; and the more integrated the world economy — that is, the more readily supplies from one country are available to others — the less these chances are. Where quotas are used, the foreigner, so far from paying, may share in the consequential rise in price. It is true that a country introducing trade restrictions that

87

substantially diminish its purchases from abroad may be able to sustain a higher exchange rate and turn the terms of trade slightly in its favour. But any gain of this kind is likely to be more than offset by the substitution of higher cost domestic products for cheaper imported supplies.

5.33   There is also a tendency to exaggerate the value of protection as a means of defending a high standard of living against the inroads of goods made by low-cost labour in developing countries. The only secure defence of a high standard of living is high productivity, including skill in innovating and keeping pace with technical change. It is not possible by any form of protection to prevent industry from locating itself where costs are lowest, and that is unlikely always to be where labour is cheapest. Some countries may refuse to take advantage of the lower costs and deny entry to imports, but other countries will have no reason to exclude them or will take a different line and admit them. There can be no guarantee that the emergence of more industrial countries will leave standards of living elsewhere unaffected. The example of Japan goes to show, however, that newcomers may help rather than hinder a rise in living standards. It does not help matters to refuse to trade with the newcomers: it simply makes matters worse. Industrial countries need to reconcile themselves to the rise of an increasing number of competitors in traditional industries and find ways of profiting from it by adjusting themselves to that expectation.

5.34   In the meantime the industrial countries need to recognise how much they depend on the developing countries as markets. If trade within Western Europe and between the United States and Canada is excluded, no less than 48 per cent of exports from the industrial countries go to developing countries, of which 31 percentage points go to the non-oil exporting countries.[15] As Table 5.1 shows, not only have the developing countries been increasingly important customers over the past decade: their imports of manufactures from the industrial countries have grown faster than the flow of exports in the reverse direction and in 1980 were nearly four times as large. The industrial countries may be reluctant to absorb all the manufactures the developing countries could supply: but their sales of manufactures to the developing countries, on four times that scale, are dependent on the willingness and ability of the developing countries to pay for them. If imports from the latter are limited, there are bound to be repercussions on what they can afford to buy: the fall in imports will tend to be balanced by a corresponding fall in exports. Indeed, since the developing countries are only able to go on borrowing if their prospects of expanding their exports remain healthy, damage to these prospects may cut off loans and enforce a larger contraction in imports of manufactures than the initial limitation of their exports. The industrial countries would then suffer a net contraction in the demand for their manufactures, instead of enjoying an expansion. But the matter does not rest there. For when a low-cost producer is denied access to the home markets of industrial countries he can concentrate on the foreign markets to which they sell and under-cut their exports unless they take on the burden of export subsidies. It is too easily assumed that the only form of import penetration that need cause concern is of the domestic market: third markets may be at least as important.

TABLE 5.1
Industrial Countries' Trade in Manufactures with
Developing Countries
(billion dollars)

Trading partner	1973	1977	1980
Traditional oil exporters			
Exports	13.25	57.20	82.30
Imports	0.65	0.95	2.00
Net exports	12.60	56.25	80.30
Other developing countries			
Exports	40.15	76.35	144.90
Imports	15.10	30.70	56.50
Net exports	25.05	45.65	88.40
All developing countries			
Exports	53.40	133.55	227.20
Imports	15.75	31.65	58.50
Net exports	37.65	101.90	168.70

For country groupings, see Appendix 3.

Source: GATT, *International Trade 1980/81* (Table A22).

5.35   Protection, finally, is not simply a matter of commercial advantage. It can have repercussions on all aspects of policy and affect international relations profoundly for good or ill. Whether it is exercised directly through tariffs and quotas or indirectly through investment and industrial policy, government intervention politicises trade. In pursuit of immediate national advantage, the government becomes involved in the whole span of international transactions and exposed to political pressures that may have little to do with national advantage. The more detailed its involvement, the greater the likelihood that the cumulative consequences of its actions will fail to be taken into account and that discrimination of one kind or another will be unavoidable. The danger of antagonising other countries and inviting retaliation or bringing on a trade war is much enhanced. That danger may be mitigated if protection is held in check by internationally agreed rules. But if the effect of the rules is merely to divert protection from the familiar, transparent and easily monitored forms that it used to take, to highly discriminatory and frequently unpublished limitations on access to markets, international friction will continue to mount.

References

1. Richard Blackhurst, Nicolas Marian and Jan Tumlir, *Adjustment, Trade and Growth in Developed and Developing Countries,* GATT Studies in International Trade No.6, September 1978; UNCTAD, *Protectionism and Structural Adjustment in the World Economy* (TD/B/888), 15 January 1982; and OECD, *The Case for Positive Adjustment Policies: a Compendium of OECD Documents, 1978/79,* June 1979.

2. Robert McNamara, "The High Cost of Protectionism", *Institutional Investor,* September 1979.

3. M. E. Morkre and D. G. Tarr, *Effects of Restrictions on United States Imports, Five Case Studies and Theory,* Staff Report of the Bureau of Economics to the Federal Trade Commission, June 1980. In each case the costs of protection to consumers significantly exceeded the benefits to producers. Another estimate, which included the effect of quotas as well as tariffs, put the cost to United States consumers of import restraints on clothing at between $2 billion and $4 billion a year in 1978. (See D. Keesing and M. Wolf, *Textile Quotas Against Developing Countries,* Trade Policy Research Centre, October 1980, p.107.)

4. This study by the Foreign Trade Association, based in Brussels and Cologne, is summarised in D. Keesing and M. Wolf, *op. cit.,* p.107.

5. Glenn P. Jenkins, *Costs and Consequences of the New Protectionism — The Case of Canada's Clothing Sector,* Canada: The North-South Institute, July 1980.

6. The consumer cost is calculated by the Industries Assistance Commission as the gross subsidy equivalent (the increase in producers' gross revenue provided by assistance) plus the increase in the cost of imports resulting from assistance to Australian producers. In clothing in 1977-78, the average nominal rate of assistance was 76 per cent and the effective rate (taking into account the higher prices paid for Australian-made clothing) was calculated as 135 per cent. (See IAC, *Report on Textiles, Clothing and Footwear,* Canberra, 1980.)

7. This issue is discussed in T. E. Josling and D. Hamway, "Distribution of Costs and Benefits of Farm Policies", in T. E. Josling *et al., Burdens and Benefits of Farm-Support Policies,* Trade Policy Research Centre, 1972.

8. See Commission of the European Communities, *Stocktaking of the Common Agricultural Policy,* 1975.

9. These estimates are from D. Gale Johnson, *World Agriculture in Disarray,* Macmillan, 1973, p.51.

10. The amounts were $18.6 billion for dairy products, $4.7 billion for wheat and $3.7 billion for sugar. (Source: FAO, *Commodity Review and Outlook,* 1979/80, p.114.)

11. $10.6 billion for rice and $1.2 billion for dairy products. (Source: *ibid.*)

12. $2.7 billion for dairy products and $1.2 billion for sugar. (Source: *ibid.*)

13. See World Bank, *World Development Report 1981,* and C. Hamilton, "Shipbuilding: a Study in Adjustment", quoted by H. Hughes and J. Waelbroeck, in "Can Developing Country Exports Keep Growing in the 1980s?", *The World Economy,* June 1981.

14. UNCTAD, *op. cit.*

15. GATT, *International Trade 1980/81,* Table A23.

6. Preferential and Other Special Arrangements

".... the objectives of the generalized non-reciprocal, non-discriminatory system of preferences in favour of the developing countries, including special measures in favour of the least advanced among the developing countries, should be: to increase their export earnings; to promote their industrialization; and to accelerate their rates of economic growth"

Resolution 21(II) UNCTAD, New Delhi, 1968

6.1 No consideration of the extent and forms of protection would be complete without reference to the preferential and other special arrangements existing in individual markets, in favour of exports from developing countries. The most noteworthy of these are the various schemes introduced under the Generalized System of Preferences (GSP), which apply in principle to all developing countries, and the Lomé Convention which, with some exceptions and limitations, gives duty-free and quota-free trade access to the EEC for African, Caribbean and Pacific member countries (ACP). These arrangements replaced earlier preferences received by many countries from developed countries with which they had historical links; along with newer elements, they are applied to broader groups of both preference-giving and preference-receiving countries. Apart from the GSP and Lomé there are special provisions in the import tariffs of some developed countries which, while varying in detail, provide for partial remission of duty on imports of articles processed or assembled from components originating in the developed country.

The Generalized System of Preferences
6.2 At the second UNCTAD in 1968, a generalized system of non-reciprocal preferences for developing countries was agreed. The aim was to increase their export earnings, promote their industrialisation and accelerate the rate of their economic growth. Unlike the preferences

extended, on a reciprocal footing, by the United Kingdom, France, the Netherlands and others to countries with which they had historical links, all of which have now been superseded, the schemes introduced under the GSP extend preferential access on a non-reciprocal basis to nearly all the developing countries. However, they are greatly circumscribed by product exclusions, and by limitations on the preferences granted through tariff quotas, ceilings and maximum country amounts. Most schemes have a restricted coverage of agricultural products and either exclude or severely limit the preference granted to 'sensitive' products — those in which import penetration tends to be strong and in which therefore beneficiary countries have a substantial interest. All provide for unilateral termination or alteration by the implementing country without compensation for the affected parties; in GATT terminology none of the GSP concessions is 'bound'.

6.3   After detailed negotiations in OECD and UNCTAD, the GSP schemes of individual countries began to be implemented from 1971 and 1972, although the schemes of Canada and the United States had to wait until the middle of the 1970s. A pioneering scheme was introduced by Australia in the middle 1960s. The various schemes were not uniform and, for a number of reasons, the main products to benefit were manufactures and semi-manufactures. In 1976, by which time all GSP schemes were operational, GATT calculations show that, out of m.f.n. dutiable imports of agricultural products from GSP beneficiary countries amounting to $20.3 billion, only $4.6 billion qualified nominally for GSP treatment. With industrial products the proportion was very different, GSP eligible items accounting for $22.5 billion out of m.f.n. dutiable imports valued at $34.6 billion.

6.4   Among the agreed conclusions of the UNCTAD Special Committee on Preferences, that established the norms of the system, was the consideration that efforts for further improvements should be pursued in a dynamic context. What happened in practice, however, was a dilatory and defensive implementation of schemes which, because of their unilateral and temporary nature, lacked the incentive and certainty to evoke a significant increase in supplies. Also, being non-reciprocal, they were never seriously intended to involve structural adjustment in the preference-giving countries. They came replete with safeguards and prior limitations. Those products, like textiles and footwear, in which comparative advantage had already been demonstrated, were excluded from nearly all schemes at the outset. The EEC in principle included textiles in its scheme for countries that adhered to the Long-term Arrangements on International Trade in Cotton Textiles (and later the Multifibre Arrangement (MFA)), but severely restricted the benefits by a system of maximum country amounts (tariff quotas). Thus the effect in this area was largely a revenue effect, with little trade volume impact at the margin, except insofar as the GSP and the MFA combined might have favoured exports from smaller producing countries or new entrants to the trade.

6.5 Data supplied to the UNCTAD secretariat by preference-giving countries, showing the extent of utilisation of their GSP schemes, indicate that the role of the GSP in improving market access for developing countries has been small but not insignificant. The latest available data, mostly for 1980, show imports under GSP by OECD and two centrally planned preference-giving countries valued at about $27 billion, i.e. something under half the $58 billion of imports into these countries nominally eligible for GSP treatment, out of the total of dutiable imports amounting to $115 billion. Thus, roughly a quarter of m.f.n. dutiable imports are cleared under the GSP. This amounts to a little more than a tenth of total imports by these countries from GSP beneficiaries, when allowance is made for the portion of imports entering duty-free on an m.f.n. basis. In 1976, the first year when all schemes were being implemented, the comparable proportion was less than 7 per cent.

6.6 According to GATT, the trade-weighted average post-Tokyo Round preference margin for agricultural products included in the various schemes was about 8 per cent. For industrial products the margin would be about 7 per cent, or somewhat more at present as the staged m.f.n. cuts agreed to during the Tokyo Round are not yet fully implemented. Applying a factor of 8 per cent to the data presented above, which show imports cleared under the GSP amounting to $27 billion in 1980, gives a rough estimate of about $2.2 billion in terms of revenue foregone.

6.7 This is slightly less than the comparable figure in 1977, at current values, and demonstrates the declining importance of the GSP in real terms. This is particularly the case with schemes based on prior limitations. The annual increases in value ceilings in the scheme of the EEC have been less than the underlying rate of inflation, and in recent years there have been no increases in ceilings for 'sensitive' industrial products. With many tariff quotas falling short of current imports, large amounts of 'sensitive' eligible imports have failed to obtain preferential treatment under the GSP. This subjecting of incremental trade volumes to m.f.n. rates of duty must considerably detract from the effectiveness of the GSP in terms of its original objective of stimulating exports.

6.8 Various studies have been made in recent years of the dynamic effects of the GSP on trade in manufactures. While the results vary widely, depending on assumption, methodology and data sample, all show a significant impact in trade terms. This is being eroded by the lack of an inflation factor, however, in those schemes based on prior limitations expressed in value terms, by the discriminatory way in which the more successful developing country exporters are being phased out of benefits in respect of 'sensitive' products, and by m.f.n. tariff reductions. This is not incompatible with the original conception of the system from the standpoint of developed countries, as a time-bound, non-contractual, non-reciprocal arrangement under which they would give what it cost them little to give, and would take it away when appropriate. But the consequence is that, as at present constituted, the GSP is too small and too uncertain an element in investment calculations to have any very significant effect on industrialisation.

6.9 Two aspects of the picture have attracted particular attention in the past. These are the low apparent rates of utilisation of the generalized preferences nominally on offer, and the fact that most use is made of them by a comparatively small number of developing countries. The greater use of the GSP by a small number of more advanced developing countries simply reflects their greater capabilities to take advantage of the schemes. The low levels of utilisation by the less advanced developing countries highlight the need for some beneficiary countries to improve their supply response, and for complementary measures to help them in doing so. More technical and other assistance, particularly to counter the greater proportionate burden that GSP documentation and international representation sometimes impose on smaller trading countries, could help them in this regard and such assistance could be provided. More careful attention might also be given by the licensing authorities in some preference-giving countries to assure equitable access to GSP tariff quotas by new entrants.

6.10 There is a feeling among a few developing countries with a competitive industrial base that the GSP has little value for them. In the light of the increasing tendency for them to be discriminated against, either by being 'graduated' out of the GSP benefits, or by being the target of other selective measures of protection, they see the maintenance of free markets as their main concern in the world's trading arrangements.

6.11 In view of the limited benefits conferred by the GSP, the question arises whether developing countries should not give greater emphasis to securing m.f.n. tariff reductions, although this would reduce the significance of the GSP. At present the fear of erosion of preferences can be used as an excuse against m.f.n. tariff reductions for products of interest to developing countries. Yet for some developing countries, and for others in the long-run, there are greater advantages in securing m.f.n.

reductions which are bound, and are not limited, and therefore provide greater certainty. Preferences tend to impair the principle of non-discrimination in international trade policy and, generally, developing countries have a strong interest in maintaining and strengthening this principle, subject to agreed exceptions in conformity with Part IV of GATT (Appendix 1).

6.12   The lack of uniformity among the various GSP schemes, and the administrative complexity of some of them, have long been a cause for concern. While the reasons for this complexity are understood, possibilities for standardisation and simplification in future should be pursued, especially taking into account progress in related fields such as the customs valuation code negotiated in the Tokyo Round, and the current work on tariff harmonisation in the Customs Cooperation Council. There is need to move towards a uniform coverage and depth of tariff cut within the GSP. However, it must be acknowledged that the major difference in the GSP schemes is more fundamental, separating the EEC-type schemes with their prior limitations, from the US-type, comparatively open-ended schemes with safeguards based on some sort of 'competitive need' formula, or a traditional safeguard clause. Without seeming to minimise the difficulties that would lie in the way of bridging this gap, it would be desirable to move towards the more open-ended and less complex features of a US-type scheme.

The Lomé Convention
6.13   The first Lomé Convention between the EEC and the ACP countries provided for contractual, institutionalised and time-bound preferences in the enlarged EEC to be shared by eligible Commonwealth developing countries and the francophone African states associated with the original members of the EEC under the Yaoundé Convention. The more populous and generally more industrially advanced Commonwealth countries in south and south-east Asia were excluded from eligibility on grounds of incompatibility, but a Declaration of Intent on the part of the EEC envisaged utilising the mechanisms of the GSP to provide some assurance against trade deflection, in the manner indicated in paragraph 6.27 below.

6.14   The second Convention, in the same way and with an enlarged membership, now covers four main areas: trade, aid, industrial cooperation and export earnings stabilization (Stabex). The trade provisions of the Convention provide for duty-free and quota-free entry for most imports of ACP origin into the EEC. In the case of a comparatively small number of agricultural products of ACP origin which face duties and levies on importation into the EEC, the import charges are usually less than those applicable to non-ACP goods and, in some cases, they are almost entirely waived. For example, 90 per cent of the levy on beef originating in Botswana and certain other countries in Africa is remitted to the exporting countries. For a range of agricultural products that were of particular significance in the system of Commonwealth preferences, special arrangements have been made in a series of protocols to the Convention. The most important of these is for sugar. There are also protocols for rum and bananas.

6.15   However, while nearly all imports from the ACP into the EEC enter duty-free, the nominally generous access is not as substantial as it appears. For example, quantitative restrictions still apply to some imports, like beef, sugar and rum. Rules of origin remain restrictive and complex. More than three-quarters of ACP exports would enter the EEC duty-free and more than 90 per cent of their industrial exports would be eligible for GSP treatment in the absence of the Lomé Convention. The access provisions are also qualified by provisions for safeguard action.

6.16   Among the main differences between the Convention and the GSP are that the former, contractual relationship is more restricted in its membership but more beneficial in its terms, especially on the side of agriculture, as well as in providing preferences with greater time-bound certainty. On the whole, the advantages of Lomé to developing country members are potentially considerable.

6.17   Restrictive origin rules, safeguard clauses and the retention of barriers on some agricultural exports, do not alter the fact that significant preferences are provided to the ACP by the Convention. On the whole, however, the preferences do not seem to have had much beneficial effect on ACP exports. Between 1975 and 1980, when EEC imports of all products from the ACP fluctuated around 7 per cent of total EEC imports, the ACP share of EEC imports of semi-finished and finished manufactures, at just above 3 per cent, actually fell, while the share of other developing countries in the trade in these products rose from 12 to over 15 per cent. There is doubtless scope for improving the preferences, as is indicated below in the last section of this chapter, but it is obvious that supply problems are a great constraint on their effective utilisation.

Value-Added Tariffs
6.18   While not inherently preferential, other new developments in business practices and tariff structures have been of particular relevance to the prospects for manufactured exports from developing countries. Since the late 1960s there has been rapid growth in 'outward-processing' or 'offshore assembly'. These expressions refer to the assembly or processing

for re-export, under favourable tariff treatment at both ends of the trade, of components and parts originating in industrial countries. Exports arranged on this basis now average about 20 per cent of total developing country manufactured exports to the United States. The income (value-added) accruing to the developing country exporters from these activities is typically much less than the gross value of their exports, and usually less than that from an equal dollar value of traditional exports. Where traditional products like textiles, clothing and footwear face severe trade barriers in the developed countries, outward-processing offers an alternative or additional path along which developing countries seeking to initiate or accelerate industrial export growth may move. The establishment of export processing zones in developing countries, combined with the 'value-added' tariffs of developed countries, has greatly facilitated this movement.

6.19 While they have so far been concentrated in the clothing and electronics sectors, the variety of such outward-processing activities now being undertaken is extensive and growing. In general they are relatively unskilled labour-intensive activities, whether component manufacturing or processing, of a kind which can readily be segmented out of previously integrated production facilities. Transnational manufacturing and trading companies search out the cheapest sources for their requirements, either for direct purchasing from local firms or for location of their own establishments. In their quest to minimise costs, they now integrate developing countries into their global operations as suppliers not only of raw materials, as in the past, but also of particular manufactured products and processes.

6.20 The value-added tariff arrangements to be found in the tariff schedules of most industrial countries provide for duty-free re-entry or duty relief on domestically produced components which have been assembled or processed abroad. This frees the finished product of the full burden of import duties which would otherwise have to be paid on the sometimes substantial value of imported inputs, and thus encourages labour-abundant developing countries to conduct processing and assembly activities in which they possess comparative advantage. The value-added tariff reduces what would otherwise be the level of overall protection for the final product's manufacture in the industrial country. On the other hand, by lowering costs of components and assembly activities, and by providing a market for the original exported inputs, this tariff provision can enhance the profitability of the relevant industry and protect all of it other than those parts being relocated abroad. Where no import duties are to be levied on the relevant final product, whether because of GSP provisions, the Lomé Convention or zero m.f.n. rates, there are no advantages offered by value-added tariffs; outward-processing already is encouraged by freedom from trade barriers.

6.21 While most developed countries operate their own version, the best known example of these tariff provisions is that of the United States. Item 807.00 of the US tariff schedule, which accounts for over 90 per cent of US imports under these provisions, allows duty-free re-entry only of components that do not lose their physical identity in the assembled article. Item 806.30 provides for offshore processing of certain metal products, but is limited to products that are returned for further processing in the United States. Under both headings the tariff relief attaches to the components of US origin, irrespective of the nationality of the firms involved.

6.22 In 1976 the EEC adopted a common outward-processing scheme, which differs from that of the United States in certain respects. For example, the EEC provisions apply to all kinds of products and to all forms of processing as well as to simple assembly. They also require that the exporting firm be resident in the EEC, and that the components be assembled and re-exported to that company on its own account. The extent of duty remission on EEC imports differs from that in the US scheme; it depends on the import duty applicable to the inputs in question had they been imported in unincorporated form. A similar provision forms part of the Japanese arrangements.

6.23 Outward-processing has also been favoured under the MFA which authorises special and differential treatment for re-imports into a participating country of textile products which that country has exported to another participating country.

6.24 Although a system of outward-processing is likely to provide significant opportunities for expanding exports of manufactures from developing countries, it is not without shortcomings. The processing activities usually consist of a few routine operations using low-cost labour. Limited industrialisation occurs through specialisation in labour-intensive technology of single components or assembly processes, with perhaps limited opportunity for the development of entrepreneurial and industrial skills. A manufacturing process which in this way tends to be dependent exclusively on foreign inputs, may severely restrict the development of economic linkages within the domestic economy. Tariff relief on outward-processing may be one means by which otherwise high effective rates of protection on manufacturing can be mitigated. But the structure of manufactured exports from developing countries which results from these differentiated trade barriers need not coincide with that which comparative advantage or development aspirations, by themselves, would dictate.

6.25 Value-added tariffs and other provisions relating to outward-processing are not at present governed by agreed international conventions or guidelines. Some schemes are open to all; some are only available to locally-based firms. Some apply only to some sectors or types of activity; others are more universally applicable. Some such concessions are fully transparent, with public information as to their use being readily available; others are made available on a discretionary and secretive basis. The objectives of non-discrimination and transparency would be advanced by multilateral adoption of common procedures and policies regarding value-added tariffs and outward-processing. These would have maximum potential impact if their special provisions were available to all firms, within all industries. Regular reporting as to the dimensions and characteristics of their use, apart from the inherent advantages of transparency, would facilitate assessment of their overall role in the development of developing countries' industrial exports.

The Way Ahead
6.26 The apparently conflicting objectives of preferences and non-discrimination, and the trade arrangements reflecting these orientations, have been considered with a view to identifying areas for rationalization. The long-term objective must be non-discrimination. We do not start with a *tabula rasa,* but with historically determined regional preferences, and there exists a powerful rationale for the granting of general preferences to developing countries. Some countries are likely to gain more from a universal application of non-discrimination than they would lose from giving up their preferences: if, however, universal non-discrimination cannot be guaranteed, these countries cannot be expected to enjoy losing advantages which they now possess.

6.27 In spite of its limitations, to which attention has been drawn, and in the absence of a more extensive reduction of trade barriers, the GSP should be retained and improved, and consideration given to a more systematic application of its principles, by extending them to non-tariff measures, and in other ways. Apart from anything else, it has provided the mechanism, within the spirit of GATT, for some degree of 'compensation' to Asian Commonwealth countries that were excluded from eligibility in Lomé, by the opening of bilateral tariff quotas on certain products of export interest to them. Several of the GSP tariff preferences, which served to mitigate the adverse effects of the enlargement of the EEC on Asian countries, are still of considerable commercial importance in this context. Moreover, the formation of the EEC and its arrangements with EFTA has generated discrimination against all non-members, including all non-ACP developing countries. Until the GATT proves more effective in reducing m.f.n. tariffs and other restraints on exports of interest to developing countries, the GSP has a role, albeit second best, in mitigating barriers against these exports. It should be made to respond more closely to the needs of the developing countries, especially the poorer ones.

6.28   The situation where GSP preferences could be and are withdrawn unilaterally, without reference to injury or trade disruption, should be ended. These withdrawals should take place on a multilaterally agreed and uniform basis. Any eventual phasing out of GSP arrangements, for those developing countries that can continue to achieve a buoyant expansion of exports without them, should also be subject to multilaterally agreed rules. In each case, when necessary, compensatory concessions for loss of preference should negotiated.

6.29   The EEC and Japanese schemes have incorporated preferential access without limitation for the least developed countries. This principle should be adopted by other countries which have not yet done so.

6.30   The GSP should also be extended in the area of primary and pro-cessed agricultural products, without limitation, as these are the areas in which some of the low income developing countries could expect to find comparative advantage. Any resulting erosion of preferences in those countries having special preferential arrangements, such as are provided by the Lomé Convention, should be compensated by equivalent benefits in third markets.

6.31   The Lomé Convention has sought to preserve the most liberal features of former preferential trade regimes, while being made broader and less exclusive than the arrangements it replaced. In this respect it points the way ahead for preferences generally. Lomé has the advantage of tending to involve less industrially advanced developing countries and it provides them with more liberal access than is accorded by the GSP. It applies to some extent to the non-tariff area as well as to tariffs. It might thus serve as a model for wider preferential arrangements between developed and developing countries.

6.32   However, in spite of its unexceptionable intentions, the Lomé Convention has not always prevented, and may not do so in the future, the adoption of inward-looking policies by the Community. Although the free trade element is important for the ACP, the EEC, given its own economic difficulties, seems to be unprepared to encourage full advantage to be taken of the access provisions, particularly insofar as these relate to the products of labour-intensive industries like textiles and clothing. Indeed, safeguard measures have already been threatened on the few ACP exporters that have made some headway in increasing exports of these products, although they are as yet responsible for an insignificant proportion of import penetration. And, instead of adjusting in such a way as to allow freer access to processed and manufactured goods from the emerging industrial sectors of the ACP, the EEC has sought to influence investment in the ACP along lines deemed to be complementary or harmonious with the structure of European industry. In particular, this implies more favourable treatment for ACP exports within EEC-based firms. The Lomé rules of origin are also intended to exert influence of this sort.

6.33   These rules of origin allow cumulation of origin involving more than one ACP state (i.e. the ACP states are considered as being, for origin purposes, one territory). They also allow cumulation of donor country content (i.e. they allow imports from the EEC to be considered as originating products). While these are positive elements, the high levels of value added required by the rules of origin, their proscription of 'simple mixing' and 'simple assembly', combined with the provision for cumulation of donor country content, make it difficult for indigenous (as well as non-EEC foreign) enterprises to grow, on the basis of trade with the EEC, in competition with offshoots of European enterprises. The origin rules should be liberalised to make them more appropriate to the stage of development reached by most ACP countries.

6.34   At the same time there is need for caution against the bilateral and inward-looking tendencies in some regional arrangements which, if left unchecked, may impede further progress in multilateral trade liberalisation. The provisions for cumulation of EEC origin in Lomé, the value-added tariffs of the developed country markets, and the recent Caribbean Basin Initiative may each, considered in isolation, encourage increased access for the exports of beneficiary developing countries. But unless efforts are made at some stage to standardise, 'untie' and multilateralise these arrangements in favour of the less industrially advanced developing countries, they may inhibit multilateral trade liberalisation on a non-discriminatory basis. Efforts should thus be made to secure a negotiated convergence of general and regional preferences for the less industrially advanced developing countries.

7. Problems and Limitations in the International Machinery Governing International Trade

"So today the message is a difficult one but it must be put across: there is no salvation outside a generally applied system of multilateral rules and every departure from the rules, however temporary or exceptional it is intended to be, helps to weaken the system and to destroy the confidence which governments and businessmen should be able to repose in it."

Arthur Dunkel, 1982

7.1 There is widespread anxiety concerning the prospects for international trade and the adequacy of existing international institutions to deal with trade problems in the 1980s. This anxiety is shared by both developing and developed countries. It has generated proposals for immediate and relatively marginal alterations in codes and practices, and much more ambitious suggestions for major institutional reform. Anxiety has intensified with the deepening of the current severe worldwide recession and the increase of protectionism, but in fact it preceded these developments. As noted in earlier chapters, the problems emanating from the existing international institutional machinery derive from longstanding gaps in coverage and limitations in the functioning of the GATT, changes in the trading environment which have reduced the impact of GATT rules, and the widespread emergence of new forms of protectionist practice.

7.2 Nevertheless, the GATT has substantial achievements to its credit and its very existence has probably prevented much more backsliding from its founders' liberal trading ideals than there has been. The risks of reversion to inward-oriented policies, bilateral and discriminatory trade negotiations, and even trade and investment 'wars', risks which are perceived with particular clarity by the smaller and weaker trading nations, demand a major effort to restore credibility and order to the international trade regime. As the victims of increasing discrimination, the developing countries have disproportionate interest in a return to the first principles of the GATT: multilateralism and non-discrimination.

Non-Tariff Measures and the GATT

7.3   The foremost problem in the current multilateral trade regime is that, at a time when non-tariff measures (NTMs) have emerged as the most important form of trade barrier, the GATT has very limited machinery to deal with them. Where a relevant measure exists, because of the ambiguity of its drafting or the lack of objective definitions of crucial terms, it is often impossible to apply without the virtual certainty of dispute. In part, the GATT's limitations stem from the 'exceptions' to the general prohibition of quantitative restrictions (of Article XI) which were either written into its original articles or permitted by means of formal waivers later. In part, they are the product of new developments in private trade and governmental practices to which the GATT has not as yet been able to respond. The most important 'exceptions' to the GATT prohibition of quantitative restrictions, as far as the prospects for developing countries' exports are concerned, are those relating to textiles and clothing (under the MFA), the 'safeguard' clause (Article XIX), which has increasingly been honoured in the breach, and agriculture.

7.4   The greatest failure of the Tokyo Round was the breakdown of negotiations concerning the modalities of the safeguard clause (Article XIX). This was originally intended to authorise emergency action, including quantitative restrictions, when 'unforeseen developments' caused or threatened 'serious injury' to domestic producers; 'serious injury' was not defined. Its application was to be preceded by consultations and it was to be non-discriminatory among supplying countries. Originally intended to relate to 'emergencies' associated with prior tariff concessions, thereby encouraging greater liberalisation than might have been possible without such an escape clause, its use has long since been extended more widely. In recent years, the requirement of non-discrimination has discouraged resort to the clause. More and more 'safeguard' actions have ignored it in favour of quantitative restraints negotiated outside the legal framework of the GATT, particularly in the form of voluntary export restraints (VERs) and orderly marketing arrangements (OMAs), many of which were not publicly negotiated or even disclosed. The bringing of safeguard action of all kinds into the public domain and into an agreed framework of rights and obligations is undoubtedly the most important element of 'unfinished business' from the Tokyo Round. Despite considerable further consultation, negotiations on this item are still at an impasse.

7.5   The principal point at issue is that of 'selectivity' (or discrimination) in the application of the measures in question. Developing countries resisted pressure on the part of some developed countries to agree to a code which would authorise discriminatory measures against only those countries which were the source of the 'disruptive' imports. While the developed countries in question argued that non-discriminatory application would harm 'innocent parties' and give rise to widespread claims for compensation among GATT members whose trade was held to be adversely affected, the developing countries were obviously reluctant to authorise discrimination against themselves, as they had done in the Multifibre Arrangement (MFA), to their sorrow.

7.6   An effective safeguard provision, preventing or discouraging resort to OMAs and VERs outside the bounds of multilaterally agreed norms, is of the greatest importance to developing countries. To be effective, such a provision, whether a revised article of the GATT or a code, would permit emergency protection only in clearly defined circumstances, for specified periods of time, and subject to international surveillance and control. It would include a specific definition of 'serious injury' based upon economic and objectively verifiable criteria, and incorporate related provisions for the establishment of causality between 'disruptive' imports and the 'injury' in question. Such agreed terms would encourage adjustment and prevent the continued prolongation of 'emergency' protection as is at present normal.

7.7   Non-discrimination remains the only appropriate basis for an efficient and equitable regime for international trade, and 'selectivity' in the application of safeguard provisions would involve a further departure from this norm. But an effective and open safeguard system, to which resort is actually made, is so important to the further growth of exports from developing countries, that if one with the above characteristics could be agreed, a carefully controlled and temporary concession on 'selectivity' might still be in the immediate interests of these countries; it should be considered. The MFA 'model' cannot, however, be regarded as a happy, or even an encouraging, precedent in this respect.

7.8   For maximum advantage, the adoption of an improved and effective safeguard code would have to be supported by positive adjustment policies which emphasise resource redeployment and measures to encourage mobility of resources through support for retraining and relocation.

Adjustment is required on a continuing basis in response to technological change and other demand and supply factors. A strong case can be made, however, for special and additional measures to facilitate export expansion by developing countries where it can be demonstrated that adjustment problems are at least in part the product of import penetration from these countries.

7.9   The MFA within the GATT, and the plethora of VERs and OMAs outside it, are a standing reproach to the contracting parties for their inability to improve on the existing safeguard clause. Both the MFA and the multiplicity of safeguard actions must eventually be incorporated within a satisfactory and unified set of provisions for phased adjustment to altering comparative advantage, particularly as it relates to the rapidly expanding manufactured exports of developing countries.

7.10   In agriculture, the current difficulties derive from the longstanding exclusion of the sector from GATT norms. The international implications of national agricultural policies are now recognised as demanding international treatment. There is no longer any logic, if there ever was, for the treatment of agriculture as a special case.

The New Codes on Non-Tariff Measures

7.11   As the world has moved from a trading system in which the tariff was the central trade policy instrument, with other measures permitted only in exceptional circumstances, to one in which more flexible, contingent and discretionary NTMs dominate, there have been strenuous efforts within the GATT to preserve or establish some international order in the new arrangements. As has been seen in Chapter 2, a distinguishing feature of the Tokyo Round was the progress made in establishing codes of conduct for certain NTMs. These codes make a start in developing rules to provide more effective discipline, in the sense of multilaterally contracted rights and obligations enforceable by retaliatory sanctions, in the application of NTMs. They may assist in resisting protectionist pressures, or at least in setting limits to the arbitrary use of national power in the trading arena.

7.12   In negotiating the codes the difficulties of balancing the rights and obligations of countries with divergent trading circumstances were, however, such that only very limited progress was possible and there remain some highly negotiated ambiguities that need further clarification if the new GATT system is to be truly effective. That the codes only begin to deal with the problems of the new NTMs is universally recognised. How effective they will be ultimately depends upon the vigour and will of the contracting parties, including concerned developing countries, in respect of their application and development. Some of the issues arising from the implementation of the codes, as they relate to the trade of developing countries, deserve at least brief discussion.

7.13   The code on technical barriers seeks to prevent unduly restrictive effects on trade from the domestic application of product standards or testing requirements, by requiring equal treatment for imports, the use of international standards where they exist, and by establishing mechanisms for the provision of information and consultation. The special development, financial and trade needs of developing countries are specifically recognised. There are a number of provisions relating, for instance, to technical assistance and the provision of information. It will take some time for this code to be put into effect, and it will be even longer before one will be able to assess its effectiveness.

7.14   The code on import licensing procedures seeks to mitigate, and provide for scrutiny of, unduly restrictive application of licensing arrangements. While in some instances intentional delays and obstructions in licensing systems can significantly restrict trade, this code is probably also of relatively minor immediate importance for developing countries' exports.

7.15   The extremely complex customs valuation code sought to develop uniform practices and to prohibit the assignment of arbitrarily higher valuations to imports for the purpose of raising collectable duties thereon. The developing countries' difficulties with such issues as the treatment of trade between related parties (intra-firm trade) and prices offered only to the importer concerned, were eventually accommodated, and provision was made for technical assistance and more time for implementation. This code clearly will not have a significant impact on developing countries' overall market access, although in some instances it may shift the instruments of protectionist practice to more visible forms.

7.16   The code on government procurement represents only a modest step towards the application of the principle of non-discrimination to the increasingly important area of official purchasing programmes. It establishes rules regarding tendering procedures, information requirements, transparency, and the like. But apart from the almost total exclusion of services, major elements in the public procurement of goods are not at present covered. These include procurement by state or local authorities in federal systems and by quasi-governmental authorities; activities in such major sectors as transport, telecommunications, electricity generating equipment and defence; and contracts valued at SDR 150,000 or less. Government procurement policies are frequently an important element in national industrial and developmental policies — a point recognised in special provisions made for developing countries in the code — so that agreements in this sphere may be difficult, not only to achieve but also to maintain and police. There has, nevertheless, been agreement that there should be further negotiations concerning the possible widening of the scope of this code within three years of its entry into force.

7.17　What is of immediate concern to the developing countries is the element of bilateral reciprocity associated with its implementation. The code will not take effect between any two signatories without their first reaching agreement on their respective lists of purchasing entities. This gives developed countries, because of their larger markets, considerable powers to determine, unilaterally, what measures of reciprocity (in the matter of purchasing entities) would be consistent with the special and differential treatment for developing countries that is written into the code.

7.18　By far the most important of the new codes, for developing country exporters, is that on subsidies and countervailing duties (together with the related and revised anti-dumping code). This code restates the original GATT prohibitions and exceptions regarding export subsidies, with a modernised 'illustrative list' of prohibited measures, including those relating to export credit; but it also deals with subsidies introduced for domestic policy purposes to the degree that they imply subsidies on exports. Governments are authorised to impose countervailing import duties against subsidised exports from trading partners when they cause or threaten 'material injury' to the domestic industry. While it is asserted that such 'injury' is to be evaluated in terms of all relevant factors and indices, e.g. declines in output, sales, market share, profits, return on investment, etc., and that among the matters to be considered in ascertaining its source are the volume of subsidised imports, their effects upon prices for like products in the import market, and the consequent impact upon domestic producers, there is still in fact neither a GATT definition of 'material injury' nor an agreed means to determine a causal link between imports and 'injury'. This makes it possible for national legislation to differ on crucial points of interpretation and definition. Nor are there internationally agreed methods for calculating the extent of subsidy. There should be precise and multilaterally agreed means, based on economic concepts, of determining the causal link between imports and 'market disruption', 'material injury' or 'serious injury', and the extent of appropriate redress.

7.19　Both the subsidies/countervailing duties code and the revised anti-dumping code authorise intergovernmental consultations leading to contractual 'undertakings' on the part of the subsidising exporter to stop subsidising, raise prices or fix a limit on the volume of exports, on breach of which severe penalties under national legislation would be permitted. Such negotiated bilateral settlements, lacking impartial disputes settlen.. mechanisms, are a long way from the original GATT norms of openness, 'bound' tariffs, and multilateralism. These provisions, together with the ambiguity concerning key definitions of 'injury' and the generally much greater dependence of small countries upon external trade, serve to bias the trading regime inappropriately (and perhaps inadvertently) in favour of the largest and strongest.

7.20   Developing countries frequently maintain fiscal and import regimes which result in domestic prices being higher than world prices when expressed in terms of official exchange rates. Export and other subsidies are therefore frequently essential elements in overall incentive systems which do not, in fact, disproportionately encourage non-primary exporting activity. This has been to some degree recognised in the subsidies/countervailing duties code through special provisions relating to developing country trade, including freedom for a developing country not to stop subsidies on non-primary exports immediately but merely to make a "commitment" to do so, "when the use of such export subsidies is inconsistent with its competitive and development needs". The United States has unilaterally taken the position, however, that it would not extend the code's provisions — in particular, the 'injury test' — to non-signatories (it has taken the same position on the government procurement code, excepting, however, the least developed countries). This position renders the m.f.n. provisions of the code conditional and reciprocal. Developing countries have been dissatisfied with the 'injury test' provisions and reluctant to take on some of the required obligations. Already, in a dispute with India, in which countervailing duties were applied to subsidised exports of industrial fasteners, the United States has demonstrated the discretionary and ambiguous elements of the code by unilaterally withholding its provisions even from a signatory developing country.

7.21   It is, in any case, clear that the existence of the subsidies/countervailing duties code has not prevented the major developed countries from paying substantial subsidies to industries such as motor vehicles and steel. Moreover, export subsidies on agricultural products have become the subject of major disputes among the developed countries since the code was written, suggesting that it might have weakened rather than reinforced the relevant provisions of the GATT in this sector. It seems fair to say that a sufficiently detailed and practical framework of rights and obligations has

111

yet to emerge in this code. Where protective action under Article XIX or the codes is taken, the burden of proof in respect of 'market disruption', 'injury', etc. and the obligation to demonstrate the causal link between imports and these phenomena (i.e. to show that such action is justified within the agreed rules) should be on the importing, not the exporting country.

Clarification, Disclosure and Litigation

7.22   It has been seen that many of the most important terms employed in the new GATT codes, key articles of the GATT itself (notably Article XIX — the safeguard clause) and the MFA, remain undefined. The result is that countries are free to impose trade barriers on the basis of their own national interpretations and definitions of such matters as 'material injury' (anti-dumping and countervailing duties), 'serious injury' (the safeguard clause), and 'market disruption' (the MFA). Similarly, there are no detailed agreements as to the ways of establishing the appropriate duties or other restraints in specific cases. The governments of the importing countries are not at present required to establish their case before any international surveillance body, except to a very limited extent in the MFA. Rather, the burden of proof is upon the exporting countries to show that the interpretations in question are incorrect. For most developing countries this burden is very difficult to assume. It is therefore a matter of the utmost importance that international norms, with specific economic analytical content, are established in respect of these terms and issues.

7.23   A great deal of further effort in the GATT is clearly required to clarify and interpret the rules that exist, as well as, where possible, to extend the GATT's scope (both in terms of activities that need to be covered and the types of protective device that remain at present outside the GATT). The aim in this process must be to establish rules that uphold and strengthen in practice the principle of non-discrimination and promote greater transparency in protective measures that are found to be necessary by the contracting parties. This work need not and should not wait for further rounds of trade liberalisation or negotiations for substantial reductions in quantitative restrictions. The GATT Ministerial Meeting could give much needed impetus to this effort.

7.24   The task of clarifying and improving the rules is obviously not simply a matter of improved drafting or of further negotiations on specific points of detail. Also required is agreement on underlying issues and a general improvement in the negotiating framework. Some of the ambiguities in the existing rules reflect the fact that divergent positions could only be superficially accommodated, or that the issues could be settled only in bilateral negotiations with respect to specific situations.

7.25   The instruments of the new protectionism are more flexible, contingent, and *ad hoc* in their application, than are m.f.n. tariffs which are 'bound' within the GATT. They are also frequently much less obvious and visible than are such trade barriers as tariffs or even many 'traditional' types of quantitative restriction. The constant changes, increased complexity and reduced transparency of many of the NTMs which are now in frequent use have added substantially to the difficulty of monitoring, surveillance, and assessment of effects. They have also greatly raised the cost to traders of acquiring relevant information concerning market access, at the same time as they have increased uncertainty on the question. The rising importance of these new protectionist NTMs puts a new premium on the need for governmental notification and transparency in respect of measures likely to affect international trade. Information, monitoring, and analysis in the sphere of trade barriers — particularly those affecting the exports of developing countries which have the least capacity to acquire their own information — are at present inadequate.

7.26   Transparency and surveillance activities should be assisted by the provision, within each developed country, of a public forum at which those who wish to maintain or impose protective barriers, explain their purpose and the proposed form of any new barrier. Those who expect to be adversely affected should have the opportunity to argue for levels and forms which will impose the least cost upon them.

7.27   Such arrangements are already to be found in some countries. For example, in Australia, increases in protection are generally not granted without a public inquiry at which all parties (including foreign exporters) have the opportunity to appear, and over the last decade or so the Australian Industries Assistance Commission has publicly reviewed all levels of protection. Reports are published for all inquiries and all decisions are widely publicized. The Commission's *Annual Report* and other publications give detailed and highly professional calculations of the extent and costs (to Australia) of its own protection. Somewhat similar arrangements exist in the United States and New Zealand.

7.28   Data collection on NTMs is at present conducted by the secretariats of GATT, UNCTAD and the IMF, among others. There exist important precedents for GATT/UNCTAD collaboration in activities of relevance to developing countries' trade, particularly in the sphere of technical assistance. (Indeed Article XXXVIII (section 2b) of the GATT specifically authorises such cooperation.) Such collaboration should be actively encouraged. A programme of monitoring, surveillance and assessment of NTMs erected by the developed countries (or at least the major ones) against exports from developing countries is needed. This, too, is an obvious area for fruitful cooperation. A joint GATT/UNCTAD work programme should therefore be established as a matter of the highest urgency. The trade barriers to be monitored need not be confined to those at present explicitly notified to the GATT. Rather, the monitoring and surveillance exercise could be undertaken by the GATT and UNCTAD secretariats acting jointly, with the cooperation of other agencies, through a systematic process of investigation, in pursuit of multilaterally agreed objectives of increased transparency. The results should be regularly and publicly reported, perhaps in a manner analogous to that of the IMF's *Annual Report on Exchange Restrictions.* An alternative possible model is the UN Food and Agriculture Organization's published material on developments in various commodity markets. Increased transparency is a necessary first step toward reduction of the costs of the new protectionism to the developing countries.

7.29   The relative disadvantage of the smaller and weaker trading nations within the emerging trade regime does not merely concern a lack of information. While increased transparency and the regular provision of information would greatly assist developing countries in their trade and investment planning, they could still be severely and unnecessarily limited in their capacity to take advantage of trading opportunities by the high costs of making their case. Where trade barriers are contingent and dependent, in part, on the findings of courts and tribunals concerning the extent of export subsidy, the degree of 'injury', and the like, or upon the special pleading of particular firms or industries, the interests of the developing countries, and particularly of their smaller, nationally-owned firms, may be very inadequately represented. In some instances, the costs of litigation and representation can exceed the possible gains from the (quite uncertain) prospect of successful advocacy. The establishment of a 'legal aid' service should be considered through UN, GATT, Commonwealth or other auspices, to assist the most disadvantaged in making their case in circumstances where significant trading interests are at issue.

Bargaining, Reciprocity and Dispute Settlement

7.30   While the GATT is a multilateral instrument, its traditional *modus operandi* has been bilateral bargaining. From its inception a major principle in the tariff bargaining process has been reciprocity. At the same time, however, the results of the bilateral bargaining process have been applied, as a matter of principle, on a non-discriminatory (m.f.n.) basis.

7.31   Developing countries and the small developed countries have often complained that in the negotiating process in the GATT, particularly in the multilateral trade negotiations (MTNs), they play only a marginal role and because of this their interests are not adequately represented. In these negotiations bargaining takes place mainly among the major countries and the agreed results are then given general application. These procedures effectively discriminate against smaller and poorer countries with little bargaining power, and have contributed to the relatively more limited reductions of trade barriers against some of the major manufactured exports of developing countries noted in Chapter 3. It is important to consider improvements in negotiating procedures in any future MTNs as well as in other GATT fora.

7.32   The GATT m.f.n. clause (Article I) is set out in the unconditional form. That means that a GATT signatory gets, as a matter of right, the benefit of tariff concessions, and of other concessions regarding import regimes, which any other GATT signatory accords, perhaps as a result of negotiation with only a limited number of other GATT countries. This is in contrast with the pre-GATT conditional form of the m.f.n. provision which required some reciprocity from each participant in the system for each new concession.

7.33   Moreover, Part IV of the GATT (which deals specifically with trade and development and whose provisions are set out in Appendix 1) stipulates that the developed contracting parties do not expect reciprocity for the commitments they make to reduce or remove tariffs and other barriers to the exports of less-developed contracting parties. Thus, the less-developed contracting parties are not expected, in the course of trade negotiations, to make contributions which are inconsistent with their individual development, financial and trade needs, taking into consideration past trade developments. The latter formulation was employed in the Declaration which launched the Tokyo Round; but reciprocity and the conditions in which it is appropriate are matters for unilateral interpretation.

7.34   Regrettably, there has been, in fact, a pronounced drift towards reciprocity and the pre-GATT form of conditional m.f.n. in negotiations for codes on NTMs, even though each of these codes provides for some sort of differential and more favourable treatment for developing countries. One of the most striking features of these codes, apart from the start they make on controlling certain modern forms of protection, is their incorporation of a graduated form of bilateral reciprocity. Quite apart from the graduated response now being required of developing countries, there is a new element of bilateral reciprocity in the codes applying between developed countries themselves. This is by no means a new concept in historical terms, but it is somewhat at variance with the course of recent developments in GATT concerning tariffs.

7.35   The code on subsidies and countervailing duties, discussed above (paragraph 7.18), best illustrates the way in which the GATT has been moving towards a bilateral concept of reciprocity, in keeping both with the practice in the 1930s and with certain concepts in bills now pending in the US Congress. While acknowledging the need of developing countries to use subsidies, including export subsidies, the code provides that "a developing country signatory should endeavour to enter into a commitment to reduce or eliminate export subsidies when the use of such export subsidies is inconsistent with its competitive and development needs". This and the following supporting clause are question-begging and have led to disputes. As stated earlier, the United States, the main trading country with an articulated countervailing policy, has taken the position that it would not extend the 'injury test' to countries which did not sign the code and that a developing country signing the code had to enter the required commitment. Similarly, the code on government procurement has reinforced the concept of bilateral reciprocity by requiring agreement on respective lists of purchasing entities between any two signatories.

7.36   Demands for bilateral reciprocity inevitably leave individual developing countries in a weak bargaining position since the developed countries, because of their larger markets and economic power, are in a position to determine, almost unilaterally, what measures of reciprocity would be consistent with the 'special and differential' treatment that is to be accorded to the particular developing country.

7.37   Disputes settlement under the existing international machinery is also essentially a bilateral matter. The GATT has traditionally been concerned with the containment of disputes and the seeking of bilateral accommodations among the contracting parties which can preserve the overall balance of advantage from participation, rather than with adjudication or punishment of transgressors. Its mechanisms for disputes settlement involve independent panels which operate in closed session, are highly vulnerable to political influence, and are ultimately powerless. It has even proved difficult to release reports with which one of the parties to the dispute disagrees. There are no effective mechanisms to follow up the decisions of panels.

7.38   With the recent burst of complaints which have been taken to the GATT, and the probable increase in the number of GATT 'cases' which will follow from the implementation of the new codes, there is bound to be increasing interest in disputes settlement procedures and follow-up. An important first step in the strengthening of these procedures, one which is in the particular interest of the weaker trading countries, is to open them to public scrutiny. Transparency should be no less an important objective in this part of the international trade regime than it is in others.

The International Institutional Framework

7.39   A welcome start was made in the Tokyo Round to remove some of the formal deficiencies of the GATT system; but it had only limited success. A negotiating group was set up to review the international framework of rules in which world trade is conducted. The group, however, was concerned not with a general review of all the articles but only with those which permitted some scope for developing countries to be accorded 'special and differential' treatment. (In this connection it made some advances in disputes settlement procedures and in legitimising exceptions from two basic GATT principles — non-discrimination and reciprocity.) It is clear, however, from the present degree of malfunction in the international trading system that greater attention needs to be given to its adaptation to evolving circumstances and, in particular, to giving more practical effect to the GATT declarations relating to trade policies affecting the rate of economic progress in the developing countries.

7.40   In a world where the dynamics of technology and economic development are creating rapid changes in comparative advantage, it is extremely doubtful that a legalistic and narrowly-based approach, such as that embodied in the GATT, while essential, is sufficient to deal with the complex problems of adjustment faced by a variety of trading partners. The articles of the General Agreement are essentially concerned with trade, without taking account of the frequent need for industrial and other structural adjustment which is associated with it. The failure of the GATT to prevent increased protectionism in textiles and the proliferation of other restrictive sectoral arrangements may reflect a collapse of confidence by governments in the ability of their economies to adjust to competitive pressures, under the terms and timetables of the usual approaches. More optimistically, it may be that the present institutional arrangements do not properly reflect the continuing collective governmental interest in restraining individual countries in their trade policies.

7.41   The limitations of the GATT with regard to structural adjustment arise partly from its origin, when most of the chapters in the Havana Charter, including those on employment, restrictive business practices, and inter-governmental commodity agreements, were jettisoned. They were later taken up by other agencies, particularly UNCTAD. These bodies, however, are primarily consultative fora and their operational procedures are not always conducive to the negotiation of legally binding rights and obligations, as is possible in the GATT. Moreover, while providing a broader perspective to trade matters and more universal participation, they do not seem to have developed a fully integrated approach with the inter-linked issues of structural adjustment.

7.42 On the other hand, for reasons already mentioned, as well as on account of its lack of universality (which may be inherent in a contractual arrangement), the GATT by itself cannot at present adequately deal with the broader issues of international economic policy relating to trade questions. Nevertheless, its Consultative Group of Eighteen could perhaps play a more useful role in this respect than it has done so far. For example, in view of past experience, it seems unlikely that the safeguard clause could be adequately developed from its present narrow concern with temporary difficulties, without a much broader consensus on criteria and mechanisms for predictable and equitable adjustments to shifts in internationl comparative advantage. There is therefore a clear need to establish joint machinery, linking GATT, UNCTAD and other international agencies, to discuss protectionism and structural adjustment, including the policy framework for agricultural, industrial and other sectors, which could lead to, and facilitate, negotiation of specific rights and obligations in appropriate agencies. This might involve an eventual merger of some of the existing agencies if that was considered to be the best way to promote a comprehensive and action-oriented approach to problems of trade and development.

7.43 As a first step, a joint programme should be launched by appropriate agencies to monitor and assess protectionism and adjustment in both agriculture and industry, with special attention directed to NTMs. Some elements of such a programme have been suggsted above.

7.44 A dilemma in all international arrangements and agencies is that their continued effective functioning is ultimately dependent upon support from the major trading powers. If the complexion of current arrangements were to alter in such a way as too severely to prejudice the actual or perceived interests of the United States and the EEC, for instance, they could well go their own way in trading matters to an even greater extent than they already do within the GATT system. To some degree there is already a tendency for some of the developed countries to take general trade and investment issues first to the consultative processes of the EEC or the OECD rather than to more universal multilateral fora, a tendency which has increased in recent years and which should be resisted. The credibility of the international trade machinery depends upon its acceptability and use by all of its formal adherents, as well as on the greater 'relevance' of its provisions and the universality of its participation.

7.45 Institutional improvements, such as those suggested above, could make an important contribution to overcoming protectionism. In the present context of widespread economic difficulties they may constitute the only feasible avenue for multilateral progress. To put this in proper perspective, however, it must be said that while international rules and institutions can help, they are no substitute for governmental actions and decisions. Multilateralism, non-discrimination (except for what is agreed multilaterally), transparency and predictability — particularly in respect of NTMs, and consistent with special and differential treatment accorded to the developing countries — should be acceptable to all national governments as principles to govern international trade in agricultural and industrial products and in services, as well as providing a basis for lowering trade barriers.

8. Summary and Recommendations

"The growth of world trade in all its facets is both a necessary element for the growth of each country and a consequence of that growth. We reaffirm our commitment to strengthening the open multilateral trading system as embodied in GATT and to maintaining its effective operation. In order to promote stability and employment through trade and growth, we will resist protectionist pressures and trade-distorting practices. We are resolved to complete the work of the Tokyo Round and to improve the capacity of the GATT to solve current and future trade problems."

Declaration of Western Economic
Summary, Versailles, June 1982

Summary
I

8.1   The slowdown in economic growth over the past decade has had its inevitable repercussions on the expansion of international trade. After 1973 this proceeded at less than half the rate of the previous decade and in the last two years it has virtually come to a halt.

8.2   The trade of most developing countries held up better in volume than that of the developed countries, the main exceptions being the OPEC countries (which, however, had the benefit of much higher prices) and the poorer developing countries (which, on the contrary, suffered a swing in the terms of trade against them). There was also a large expansion in the 1970s in exports of manufactures, concentrated on a small group of developing countries but allowing many others to reduce their dependence on a few staple commodity exports (or even a single one) with volatile prices. At the same time, the developing countries conducted an increasing share of their total trade with one another and a diminishing share with the developed countries. Their main markets, however, continue to be in the developed countries which in turn find in the developing countries an important and expanding market for their exports.

121

8.3   On the whole, the developing countries, with the important exception of the poorer ones, survived the first oil shock of 1973-74 remarkably well. They had begun to make rapid headway in world markets for manufactures and several of them were poised for a more broadly based expansion. Even so, their share of the market in developed countries remained small, averaging about 9 per cent of total imports of manufactures and 3 per cent of the consumption of them.

8.4   Now, however, the outlook for the trade of the developing countries gives grounds for serious concern. The rate of expansion has fallen sharply over the past two years. Markets in the OPEC countries are no longer booming and markets elsewhere are stagnant; migrant workers from the other developing countries are less in demand and their remittances have ceased to grow; the terms of trade of the oil-importing countries have become steadily less favourable. The banks are less ready to lend, the inflow of new capital is less assured and leaves less to spare for new investment; moreover, the bill to be paid in interest charges is a great deal more formidable. All this comes on top of a major change in the economic climate and a devastating slowdown in economic activity throughout the world that blurs the market signals to which investment responds and makes it far harder for the developing countries to decide which way to turn in planning the future of their economies.

8.5   To make matters worse, the expansion that has been taking place in the trade of the developing countries is contingent on a freedom of access to markets in the developed countries that has been steadily curtailed. The growth in their trade, with which their entire development is closely linked, cannot be resumed at the rate necessary for that development unless the drift to protectionism is arrested and reversed. There is a very real danger that protectionism and world depression may feed on one another.

8.6   The new barriers to trade, largely outside international rules, which have grown up in the developed countries apply with special force to the manufactured exports of the developing countries and are highly discriminatory. At the same time, restrictions on trade in agricultural products, which have all along been largely denied international control and surveillance, continue unabated.

II

8.7   There is a considerable gap between the international trading regime as it was envisaged in 1948 when the GATT was negotiated and the way it now operates. On restrictive business practices, direct foreign investment, intra-firm trade, the rapidly growing trade in services, government involvement and many other prominent features of modern trading relationships, the GATT is silent. No serious efforts were made to include agricultural trade in the successive negotiating rounds of the GATT until the Tokyo Round in 1973, and quantitative restrictions on agricultural products were exempted from the start. There were no rules governing domestic industrial, regional or environmental policies, which increasingly impinge on international trade, and the tendency in practice has been to subordinate international obligations to the needs of domestic policies, as is specifically authorised in respect of the agricultural sector.

8.8   The original multilateral and non-discriminatory GATT model has also been buffeted by the realities of trading blocs and their associated partners which discriminate in favour of their members in a way contrary to the original spirit of the GATT. Above all, the developing countries, although accorded special preferential arrangements in some parts of the world trading system, have been subject to discrimination of the reverse kind in other parts of the system and have not been treated as equal trading partners.

8.9   Non-tariff measures (NTMs) have emerged as a major challenge to the entire GATT system. First of all, there has been increased use of formally permissible instruments of non-tariff protection, particularly in agriculture; there is now hardly a major agricultural product supplied by the developing countries in competition with developed countries for which the world market is not undermined or distorted by subsidised exports or concessional sales from surplus stocks of developed countries. The EEC, for example, has become the world's second largest exporter of sugar after Cuba and of beef after Australia.

8.10   Secondly, authorised NTMs within the GATT are increasingly discriminatory and selective: the most notable example is the Multifibre Arrangement (MFA) which discriminates explicitly against imports from developing countries of products of high importance to them in the early stages of industrialisation.

8.11   Thirdly, there has been increasing resort to new instruments of governmental protection such as orderly marketing arrangements and 'voluntary' export restraints, as well as import levies, direct and indirect export subsidies, and other forms of discretionary intervention. Deprived of the tariff weapon by the success of GATT in reducing industrial tariffs, these countries, in their anxiety to protect some manufacturing activities, are now resorting to the same wide range of NTMs as they introduced in earlier decades to protect agriculture. These measures, unlike the tariffs for which they are a substitute, represent a relative breakdown of order and automaticity and are usually accompanied by *de facto* discrimination among trading partners.

8.12   Thus a high proportion of trade takes place on a basis other than that of m.f.n. Discrimination is found both at a general level as between members of different trading blocs and selectively in respect of particular countries and industries. There is wholesale abuse or evasion not only of GATT principles but even of prescribed GATT rules, particularly in respect of quantitative restrictions; there is growing resort to NTMs of a kind for which there are no GATT rules. Bilateralism has gained at the expense of the envisaged multilateral approaches to trade negotiation, policy debate and disputes settlement. As NTMs have proliferated, the transparency of trade barriers has been reduced, making monitoring, surveillance, and assesssment of effects considerably more difficult. In general, much higher proportions of international trade are being 'administered' and 'managed', both by governmental and by private transnational actors, than the original GATT negotiators anticipated. Where discretion replaces rules, the weakest invariably lose most. In consequence of these and other developments there has recently emerged a popular climate of increased legitimacy for protectionist pressures and arguments in the developed countries.

8.13   Temporary balance of payments pressure, high unemployment and slower growth may help to explain the recent resurgence of protectionist pressures in these countries. But as has been seen, the degree of malfunctioning in the present world trade regime has deeper roots than these. The particular characteristics of current protectionist policy measures suggest that they are the product of more fundamental influences, including changes in world trading patterns and in the way international trade is conducted and perceived. There must therefore be careful consideration of the requirements of an effective international trading and investment order that takes the new realities more satisfactorily into account.

III

8.14   The most unfortunate feature of developed countries' agricultural protection policies is the almost universal reliance upon price support in order to stabilise domestic markets and farmers' incomes. Domestic policies, influenced by political pressures, have led to prices which are usually very high in relation to those on world markets; an array of measures has been adopted to insulate domestic markets from international competition. These prices encourage output to exceed domestic requirements, and the high levels of subsidies required to dispose of surpluses in world markets disrupt these markets. They aggravate instability and distort production, discouraging it in countries with lower costs of production. Of all forms of protection these are the most damaging to world markets. Direct income payments to groups of uncompetitive farmers, whom domestic policy requires be kept in farming, would minimise the disruptive effect of protection on trade. But consideration of alternatives can make little progress as long as national agricultural policies are exempted from international scrutiny.

8.15   Although tropical products do not usually compete with domestic production in the developed countries, they are still subject to trade restrictions which burden exports from developing countries.

8.16   Tariffs remain an important obstacle in relation to processing in developing countries, and the degree of effective protection was frequently unchanged or even increased when tariff cuts on primary products were made in the Tokyo Round. Effective tariff protection tends to be higher for processing activities in which the developing countries have a comparative advantage. The same is true of non-tariff barriers. The relaxation of such protection could be of great benefit to developing countries that are not yet in a position to export labour-intensive manufactures, since there is great scope for additional export earnings through the processing of raw materials.

8.17   After the conclusion of the Tokyo Round reductions, developed country tariffs will no longer constitute a critical barrier to trade in most manufactures, but they will still exceed 10 per cent in textiles and clothing. Trade in this sector, however, is regulated by the MFA which imposes ceilings on permitted rates of growth of imports into participating countries from 'low-cost' suppliers through a series of bilateral negotiations. It is the experience of the MFA and its related bilateral negotiations, with expanding country and product coverage, diminishing provision for growth, increasing complexity and rigidity and apparent permanence, that is contributing substantially to the growing disillusion of developing countries with the international trading system.

8.18   The impact of protectionism by developed countries in other sectors of manufacturing varies. Manufactures considered 'sensitive', though not to the same extent as textiles and clothing, include footwear, plywood and pulpwood, certain electrical and electronics goods, and some metal products. For some products, such as motor vehicles, steel and chemicals, NTMs are for the present directed mainly or entirely at other developed countries; for others, such as sports goods and musical instruments,

125

protection has been in the form of tariffs and does not seem to have had much dampening effect on the growth of imports. For others still, including many electrical goods and components, the industry has "internationalised" itself under sub-contracting and other intra-firm arrangements so that protectionist pressures have generally been resisted. There are in addition many manufactures, notably in various branches of the engineering sector, in which tariff protection by developed countries is relatively low and NTMs virtually non-existent; in these areas spontaneous market adjustment has allowed developing countries to take full opportunity of their comparative advantage to develop exports.

8.19 In service industries, NTMs of various kinds, including regulatory practices affecting the rights of establishment and market access, are applied by most countries. Because of a lack of attention in the past, however, it is not yet clear what kind of policy developments and international rules would best suit the particular needs of developing countries.

IV

8.20 There have generally been strong links between the growth of developing countries' exports and that of their economies, and few would doubt that restricting exports inhibits growth. Whatever development strategies are adopted, access to external markets is important to the great majority of developing countries and vital to those with small populations. Protection causes them costs, both immediately through a direct loss of potential foreign exchange earnings, and in the long-term through retarding or frustrating the necessary structural transformation of their economies.

8.21 Available data indicate that increases in the 'new' forms of protection by developed countries from around 1974 have had significant effects on developing countries' exports, not least in a marked slackening in their penetration of developed country markets for manufactures. Their total market share during the 1970s never exceeded 3 per cent, and after rising at about 13 per cent annually during 1970-74, it grew much less rapidly thereafter; for the decade as a whole the average annual increase was only 8 per cent. The deterioration in the relative position of developing countries' exports was especially marked in the case of clothing, after market access had been tightened considerably as a result of restrictive agreements negotiated bilaterally by participants in the MFA. One estimate suggests that developed country clothing imports from developing countries would have been around 90 per cent (about $10 billion) greater in 1980 if the 1968-76 relation between developed countries' income and their imports from developing countries had been maintained. On the same basis, the increase in imports of textiles would have been around 25 per cent (over $1 billion).

8.22　The deterioration in access was less marked for primary products, but the severe restrictions from which trade in agricultural and processed products was already suffering, particularly from NTMs, meant that some developing countries had for many years been foregoing large amounts in potential foreign exchange earnings. It has been estimated that a halving of OECD barriers to imports of food products would have raised imports from developing countries by at least $3 billion annually (in 1977 dollars), which is over a tenth of the food exports of these countries at that time. As far as processed products are concerned, the often severe degree of tariff escalation in developed countries has also had considerable adverse effects on the development of the countries in which the products originate. Removing tariffs on imports of eight processed products, for example, would according to one estimate have increased the value added in developing country processing activities by over a fifth.

8.23　The costs of protection to developing country exporters vary with the types of barrier they face. Costs would be minimised if the objects of protection were achieved by means of assistance not linked to the production of particular goods. If such a link is deemed necessary, production subsidies would be better than tariffs, and tariffs better than the variable levies applied to trade in many agricultural products and the various quantitative restrictions of the 'new' protectionism on manufactures. If there is not a reduction in all forms of protection, governments of developing countries may be driven into adopting more inward-looking and inflexible trade regimes in which dynamism, innovation and enterprise will be constrained and rapid development unlikely to be achieved.

V

8.24　Protection, however well intentioned and whatever its purpose, exacts serious costs in the countries which impose it. Thus the immediate benefits accruing to protected interests have to be set against the costs to other domestic interests and, in the long-term, to those protected as well; all these costs have also to be compared with those of alternative means of achieving the same objectives.

8.25　In the short-term protection is paid for by consumers in the form of higher prices and a reduced variety of goods. Although the costs so incurred are not easily quantifiable, estimates for developed countries point to a very large aggregate, particularly for certain temperate agricultural products and some labour-intensive manufactures. In the case of agricultural protection, the costs to consumers (including a contribution from taxpayers) in industrial countries were put at over $40 billion more than a decade ago, and they have risen since. In manufacturing, the costs to consumers in the United States of protection of just three products were estimated at over $3 billion between 1975 and 1977, while in the United Kingdom the MFA was found to have increased prices of textiles and clothing by between 15 and 40 per cent. Similar results can be quoted for many other developed countries.

8.26   If the protection involves domestic subsidies there is also a cost to the taxpayer. Subsidies to support agriculture and basic industries are estimated to have reached as much as 7 per cent of GDP in some developed countries during the 1970s, over twice the revenue from tariffs.

8.27   In the longer period, protection in developed countries also exacts costs from those producers (whether workers, employers or shareholders) who, as exporters, risk losing sales through retaliatory action abroad or, more directly, through the loss of purchasing power in the countries affected. This last point is increasingly important. For in an interdependent world, where nearly half the extra-regional exports of manufactures from North America and Western Europe go to developing countries, which have become increasingly important customers (both relatively and in absolute terms) during the past decade, the external repercussions of protective actions cannot be minimised. Costs may also be payable by the producers protected, in so far as they are locked into activities in which their productivity and income or profit are likely to be lower than they could have been in other activities; they may, in any case, eventually succumb to foreign competition and be put out of business. The existence of lower wages and inferior conditions of employment in other countries does not in itself justify protection against their goods; it is, in the main, simply a reflection of their stage of economic development.

8.28   Finally, protection exacts a cost on the whole community if it means the economy is not being operated as efficiently as otherwise would be possible. There are thus adverse long-term effects on the creation of employment, income and wealth, which arise from a weakened response to dynamic shifts in comparative advantage, an increase in structural rigidities and a consequent mis-direction of resources when competitive influences are held at bay.

8.29   Protection will not, in the final analysis, stop economic activities from locating themselves in those areas of the world where costs are lowest (though this is unlikely always to be where labour is cheapest). What is needed in those countries which are attempting to protect themselves from the effects of changes in comparative advantage is not to erect barriers to foreign goods and services but to minimise the transitional costs of structural adjustment. The incomes of those currently engaged in protected activities can best be preserved, or even raised, by giving grants or direct income supplements to individuals and enterprises in forms that encourage the movement of resources into activities more suited to the present than to the past comparative advantage of the country concerned. Ultimately, protection is not an alternative to adjustment; it will simply lead to a greater probability of trade wars between countries and increased international friction of all kinds.

VI

8.30   The trade preferences given by developed countries to developing countries, which are nowadays extended on a non-reciprocal basis, go some way towards ameliorating the trade barriers that would otherwise present a more serious obstacle to the exports of developing countries. However, these preferences are not without shortcomings. The various schemes within the Generalized System of Preferences (GSP) do not extend beyond tariffs to non-tariff barriers and are so restricted on the extent to which use can be made of them that many developing countries find them to be of strictly limited benefit, especially in view of the uncertainty surrounding their operation and continuance.

8.31   The coverage of the system in terms of imports cleared under it by OECD countries and two East European ones amounted to about $27 billion in 1980. This is roughly a quarter of their dutiable imports from beneficiary developing countries. Studies confirm that the amount of trade that would not have taken place, but for the GSP, is not negligible; but that the possible effects on investment in the supplying countries, which it would be one of the main aims to stimulate in accordance with the objective of promoting industrialisation, are greatly lessened by the way restrictions on the utilisation of the schemes are applied to incremental trade volumes, or to products that developing countries are especially good at producing.

8.32   The cost of the GSP to the Treasuries of preference-giving countries is about $2.2 billion in terms of revenue foregone. To the extent that this has dynamic effects on trade and investment it accords with the emphasis on trade rather than aid. Its uncertain continuance greatly impairs these possible effects, which could be better promoted by duty reductions on an m.f.n. basis. These would be bound against increase in GATT, whereas duty reductions under the GSP are non-contractual and can be withdrawn unilaterally without reference to injury or trade disruption. But if trade liberalisation on an m.f.n. basis cannot be assured, developing countries should not be expected to give up advantages they now possess, however circumscribed.

8.33 In these and some other respects, the Lomé Convention, being a contractual relationship, is more beneficial. It is broader and less exclusive than the preferential trade regimes it replaced, while seeking to preserve their most liberal features. It applies in principle to NTMs as well as to tariffs, so that with a few (important) exceptions, exports from the ACP countries to the EEC are quota-free as well as duty-free. Moreover, by incorporating provisions on aid, export earnings stabilisation, and industrial co-operation, the Convention addresses itself in a much more comprehensive way to the developmental and trade problems of the developing countries it is intended to assist. It is also more generous in trade co-operation in agriculture, where practically all GSP schemes are relatively weak. It is, however, geographically much more restricted in scope than the GSP.

8.34 The development of 'offshore' or 'outward' processing, by which goods from developed countries are assembled, finished or otherwise processed in developing countries for shipment back to the developed country, has been facilitated by two developments. One is the introduction of 'value-added' provisions in the import tariffs of developed countries, which allow a waiving of duty on such 'originating' goods re-entered in incorporated form. The other is the establishment of export processing zones in developing countries. Where products like textiles, clothing and footwear face severe barriers in developed countries, such arrangements offer an alternative or additional path along which developing countries seeking to initiate or accelerate industrial export growth may move.

8.35 There are, however, dangers that the rules of origin of these 'value-added' tariff provisions and of the Lomé Convention can lead to a form of industrial development in developing countries that need not coincide with that which comparative advantage or development aspirations, by themselves, would dictate. There may be a risk of the bilateral and inward-looking tendencies in some regional arrangements impeding further progress in multilateral trade liberalisation. Notwithstanding these qualifications, on the whole the advantages of the preferential arrangements, including 'value-added' tariff provisions, to developing countries are significant.

VII

8.36 Existing international machinery has proved inadequate to deal with the emerging trade problems. The limitations arise not only from continuing gaps but also from a failure to respond to new needs. Unless a major effort is made to restore credibility to the international trading regime, there is a danger of breakdown and a massive reversion to inward-looking policies and to bilateralism and discrimination.

8.37 In recent years the safeguard system — Article XIX — has been largely evaded, mainly because of the requirement of non-discrimination. The improvement of the system to enable all safeguard actions to be brought into the public domain through an agreed framework of rights and obligations is undoubtedly the most important element of 'unfinished' business from the Tokyo Round. The point at issue is the 'selectivity' or discrimination demanded by some developed countries and resisted by the developing countries. Selectivity would be a further departure from the norm of non-discrimination. However, an effective safeguard system is so important for the future growth of exports from developing countries that, if one with the required attributes could be agreed, a carefully controlled and temporary concession on the question of selectivity might still be in the interest of these countries.

8.38 An improved safeguard system requires support from positive adjustment policies. Adjustment must be a continuing process but a strong case can be made for additional adjustment assistance where problems are caused by export expansion from developing countries. The reversal of the drift to protectionism requires that 'orderly' marketing arrangements, 'voluntary' export restraints and other protective measures taken against surges of imports from developing countries be brought within the context of an improved safeguard system.

8.39 The Tokyo Round, completed in 1979, set out to consider the framework of trade and succeeded in concluding several agreements (codes) on NTMs designed to improve the rules and provide more effective discipline. The difficulties of balancing rights and obligations in this area, however, meant only limited progress in rule-making. There remain many ambiguities. Although some of the codes provide for special and differential treatment for developing countries, many problems remain in the way of ensuring benefits for these countries. The code on government procurement, for instance, entrenches bilateral reciprocity in an area where developing countries have weak bargaining power.

8.40 The code on subsidies and countervailing duties (together with the related and revised anti-dimping code) is the most important of the new codes for developing countries. But although it makes provision for the special circumstances of developing countries, its effectiveness is impaired by the lack of a clear definition of the concept of 'material injury'. In the case of this and other codes, as well as of Article XIX, there are various conceptual problems about the nature and extent of 'injury' and 'market disruption'; there is also the need to be able to establish clearly a causal link between 'injury' and imports. One major developed country has already unilaterally taken the position that it would not extend the code's provisions to non-signatory countries. Thus the m.f.n. provisions of the code are being rendered conditional and reciprocal. Moreover, experience so far has demonstrated discretionary and ambiguous elements in the code.

8.41   The interests of the developing countries and the small developed countries are inadequately represented in the GATT negotiating process. The procedures, which emphasise bilateral processes, discriminate against weaker countries. Thus although Part IV of the GATT specifically provides that developing countries should not be expected, in the course of negotiations, to make contributions which are inconsistent with their development needs, there has been an unfortunate drift to bilateral reciprocity in the codes. Bilateralism also features in the way the disputes settlement procedure operates. Its lack of transparency and high susceptibility to political influence make it ultimately ineffective.

8.42   The effective functioning of international trading arrangements is ultimately dependent upon support from the major trading partners. There is an unfortunate tendency for some of the major developed countries to take general trade and investment issues first to the consultative processes of the EEC or the OECD rather than to the more universal multilateral fora. The credibility of the international trade machinery depends upon its acceptability and use by all its formal adherents, as well as on the increased 'relevance' and greater universality of participation in its operation.

Recommendations

8.43   In the course of this survey of protectionist practices, their effects on developed as well as on developing countries, and their implications for the overall international trading system, we have considered numerous proposals for policy reforms and improvements at both the national and international level. Here we seek to draw them together in one place. These recommendations should be seen against the background of our assessment of the world trading scene.

8.44   Whilst one cannot avoid being influenced by the short-term problems of the moment, problems which are very grave indeed and which we would not want to minimise, it is important to take a longer-run view of international trading relationships and prospects. The trade policies and practices of governments today are establishing precedents for those of tomorrow. The private and public investment decisions taken in the 1980s will determine the trading patterns of the 1990s. In the inevitable focusing of policy-makers on day-to-day problems and international disputes, there may be a natural tendency for them to neglect the longer-run requirements for efficient growth, international order, and future welfare. The immediate concern with problem sectors, employment difficulties, and policies for short-term 'damage limitation', with all its attendant implications for international relationships, has an understandable internal logic. It was the same defensive logic which moved governments and decision-makers in the 1930s. It carries risks of similar outcomes.

8.45   The turmoil of the 1930s and the Second World War was followed by unprecedented international cooperative efforts at reconstructing the world economy. The international economic order established in the 1940s was not without flaws, but it achieved a substantial measure of success in terms of the aspirations of its originators. It was created by policy-makers who could see beyond the problems of the moment and retained a vision of how the world economy could and should function in the longer-run. It is a similar brand of practical and far-seeing vision which is badly needed but appears in short supply in the present disordered times. In principle, few would question the long-run desirability, in international trading relationships and regimes, of multilateralism, non-discrimination (except for what is agreed multilaterally), transparency and predictability, consistent with special and differential treatment accorded to the developing countries. Most would also agree that growth of productivity, levels of income, international equity and overall global economic welfare are likely to be significantly higher within a world trading regime which has such characteristics. In this time of disarray in the world economy and backsliding on earlier commitments to internationalist objectives, it is crucially important to restore the original beacons (or develop new ones) to guide national policy-makers through difficult times in which they are continually tempted to find what seem easier short-run solutions by turning inward.

8.46   A major element in a sustainable international trading system is a fair and equitable place for the developing countries. We have sought throughout to identify their particular stake in the future trading arrangements. In translating the more distant objectives and aspirations into the details of immediate policies it is easy either to look wildly unrealistic or, at the other extreme, to seem overcautious. We have tried to steer a middle course. We see the GATT Ministerial Meeting in November as an occasion when the appropriate tone can be set for the rest of the century. We have therefore particularly directed our recommendations towards that occasion and the work programme to which it should give rise for the decade ahead.

8.47 An essential requirement is a return to a set of agreed principles and rules applying to all international trade and providing a recognisable and ordered framework within which it can grow. In the post-war period these rules were mainly formulated and sustained in the GATT, which was highly successful in securing international agreement to reductions in tariffs on manufactured goods but has failed to check the growth of agricultural protection and the NTMs by which the trade of developing countries is increasingly limited. An orderly trading system enjoying the confidence of these countries must bring all such barriers within internationally accepted rules and procedures. Without them the developing countries have little bargaining power to employ in bilateral negotiations for the removal of trade barriers. They depend heavily for fair treatment on the observance by their trading partners of agreed rules of conduct, and the ability to publicise any breach of these rules. Apart from retaliation and such limited provision as there may be for compensation, it is difficult to devise sanctions to which the more powerful countries will agree in advance, except publicity for infringements of the rules and the disinclination of countries to be seen to be breaking rules by which they have agreed to abide.

8.48 The first step must be to address the unfinished business of the Tokyo Round. The need for action to contain protectionism in all its forms was recognised but there was no general agreement on the way of achieving this. Agricultural protection and NTMs generally have still to be brought within codes of practice capable of effective implementation. Proper surveillance of the safeguards used by importing countries is urgently required, with guidelines and procedures agreed in advance. No satisfactory mechansism has been created for the settlement of disputes, taking due account of the weak bargaining power of smaller countries and developing countries. Since protectionism is most strongly entrenched in agriculture, a decisive move towards bringing agricultural trade more fully within the purview of the GATT would signify a serious intention by governments to come to grips with the general problem of protectionism. There is need also for a more positive approach to structural adjustment as a means of reallocating resources within each country in the light of changes in comparative advantage.

8.49 We begin by considering the fundamental needs for rules and procedures and the safeguards and codes that should govern relaxation of them. We then stress the importance of transparency and publicity in rules and procedures. We discuss preferential arrangements and how these might be modified. We also make recommendations for structural adjustment and for a phased approach to liberalisation of trade in textiles and clothing and agricultural products, and end with a number of more general recommendations.

List of Recommendations

A.   Rules and Procedures
1.   The principles of multilateralism, non-discrimination (except for what is agreed multilaterally), transparency and predictability, consistent with special and differential treatment accorded to the developing countries, should be upheld and given practical support (7.23, 7.45).
2.   The growing volume of officially and unofficially administered trade should be brought under international surveillance and submitted to internationally agreed rules and procedures (2.44, 3.27).

3.   It should be recognised that multilateral review of national policies that have significant international repercussions is appropriate and necessary (3.25).

4.   Forms of protection should be chosen which, in achieving the aims of the country imposing them, occasion the least damage to exporters (3.23, 4.29).

5.   Governments should work towards a system of rules and procedures where the forms of protection and the circumstances in which it is legitimate to increase the general level of protection should be agreed in an open and multilateral forum, and except for generalised preferences, all protection should be on an m.f.n. basis (7.26).

6.   Joint machinery should be established linking GATT, UNCTAD and other international agencies, to discuss protectionism and structural adjustment, including the policy framework for agricultural, industrial and other sectors; this could lead to, and facilitate, negotiation of specific rights and obligations in appropriate agencies (7.42).

7.   These agencies should launch a joint programme to monitor and assess protectionism and structural adjustment in both agriculture and industry, with special attention directed to non-tariff measures (7.28, 7.43).

8. Practical assistance and technical support should be provided to developing countries to enable them to participate more fully in the formulation and implementation of these surveilance and control procedures (7.31).

B. Safeguards and Codes

1. The present provisions of Article XIX of the GATT should be revised to ensure that resort to all arrangements such as quotas, 'voluntary' export restraints and 'orderly' marketing arrangements is subject to greater multilateral control and discipline (3.55, 7.4).

2. The revised safeguard provisions should give clear indications of the circumstances in which protective action under Article XIX or under the codes is justifiable and should be more explicit as to the permissible scope and duration of such action; all such action should be time-bound (3.55, 7.6).

3. Existing codes governing any permitted relaxations of trade rules need to be freed from ambiguity, made precise and specific and supplemented where necessary by new codes (7.12).

4. More precise definitions based upon economic concepts should be provided for such terms as 'market disruption', 'material injury', 'serious injury', etc. (7.12).

5. There should be precise and multilaterally agreed means, based on economic concepts, of determining the causal link between imports and 'market disruption', 'material injury', or 'serious injury', and the extent of appropriate redress (7.18).

6. Provision should be made for the phasing out of arrangements such as 'voluntary' export restraints and 'orderly' marketing arrangements (7.9).

7. Where protective action under Article XIX or other articles or the codes is taken, the burden of proof in respect of 'market disruption', 'injury' etc. and the obligation to demonstrate the causal link between imports and these phenomena (i.e. to show that such action is justified within the agreed rules) should lie with the importing, not the exporting, country (7.21, 7.22).

8. Stricter disciplines are required under the Code on Subsidies and Countervailing Duties with respect to subsidies employed by the developed countries which have a strong adverse impact on the trade

of developing countries. This is necessary whether the subsidies apply directly to exports, to export credits or to domestic production (3.27).

9. The drift towards reciprocity and the pre-GATT form of conditional m.f.n. in negotiations on codes for non-tariff measures should be reversed, even if these codes provide for some sort of differential and more favourable treatment for developing countries (7.34).

10. Consideration should be given to the establishment of a 'legal aid' service for small countries to help them to pursue legitimate grievances under the GATT (7.29).

C. Multifibre Arrangement

1. The Multifibre Arrangement should be brought within the context of the rules and procedures of an improved Article XIX (3.67).

2. Developed countries should undertake a phased liberalisation of their imports of textiles and clothing from developing countries. This would require: (a) in the early stages, an increase in the annual growth in quotas and the elimination of quotas altogether for small suppliers and new entrants; (b) the eventual abolition of all quotas on these products (even if this meant a strictly time-bound increase in tariffs); and (c) a reduction within a specified time-period of their m.f.n. duties to a level much nearer to the average for all manufactures (3.67).

D. Transparency

1. Any country maintaining protective barriers or imposing new ones that are inconsistent with its obligations under international rules and procedures should have to justify its action in an open multilateral forum (4.30).

2. Countries wishing to impose such protective barriers should specify the economic aims of these barriers, not only in terms of a trade objective but also of other underlying considerations such as maintenance of employment (4.30).

3. There should be joint action by GATT and UNCTAD, with the co-operation of other agencies, to maintain and publish at regular intervals information on non-tariff barriers to trade for all countries, starting with developed countries; governments should supply all data for this to be undertaken effectively (7.28).

4. The GATT panel system for dealing with complaints and settlement of disputes should be strengthened and opened to public scrutiny (7.38).

5. National and international bodies should seek to give publicity to estimates of the cost of protection both to the countries imposing protection and to those whose trade is affected (7.27, 7.28).

6. Transparency and surveillance activities should be assisted by the provision, within each developed country, of a public forum at which those who wish to maintain or impose protective barriers should explain their purpose and the proposed form of any new barrier (7.26).

E. Preferential Arrangements

1. Efforts towards global trade liberalisation should aim in the long run at a negotiated convergence of preferential schemes, preserving the most liberal elements in each; the reduction of m.f.n. tariffs should, however, be kept in view as the preferred alternative to these schemes (6.11, 6.27, 6.31, 6.34).

2. The various preferential schemes should be improved in terms of simplicity and harmonisation of operation, and consideration should be given to their possible extension to non-tariff measures and in other ways (6.12, 6.27).

3. Preferential schemes should also be given more certainty, extended in coverage, and freed of limitations damaging to developing countries, especially the least developed among them (6.29, 6.30).

4. Any eventual phasing out of preferences for the more advanced developing countries should be subject to multilaterally agreed rules; when necessary, compensatory concessions for loss of preference should be negotiated (3.34, 6.28).

5. Policies and practices regarding 'value-added' tariffs and 'outward-processing' should be internationally harmonised and made non-discriminatory among sectors and firms; the use of such provisions should be regularly reported (6.25).

6. The rules of origin under the Lomé Convention should be relaxed to facilitate the industrial development of African, Caribbean and Pacific member countries (6.33).

F. Agriculture, Raw Materials and Processing
1.   The above recommendations concerning international machinery, rules, safeguards, codes, transparency and preferential arrangements should apply to agriculture (7.10).

2.   The immediate objectives in a phased international approach to agricultural trade liberalisation should include: (a) a standstill on current protection levels; (b) the development of codes of principles on agricultural support measures; (c) gradual improvement in access and reduction of surpluses; and (d) agreements on limits to export subsidies (3.25, 3.26).

3.   Where agricultural support is necessary, forms should be chosen which, in achieving the aims of the country imposing it, occasion least damage to exporters (3.23).

4.   The process of trade liberalisation for tropical products should be completed by the removal of remaining tariff and non-tariff restrictions (3.34).

5.   The elimination in developed countries of internal duties and taxes levied specifically on tropical products should be an object of policy (3.35).

6.   A programme should be agreed for the elimination of tariff escalation in developed countries on processed products exported from developing countries (3.49).

7.   Non-tariff measures aimed at restricting the entry of processed raw materials and foodstuffs into developed countries should be abolished (3.49).

G. Manufacturing and Services
1.   In future GATT multilateral trade negotiations, tariffs on manufactures of interest to developing countries should be cut more heavily than those on other manufactures (3.52).

2.   A comprehensive programme of studies and analyses should be established in a co-ordinated effort between GATT, UNCTAD and other international agencies, to assist governments to make an informed assessment of the extent and form of existing restrictions on services and to define possible options for any future negotiations (3.89).

3. While there is no doubt about the need to terminate inhumane labour conditions and unfair treatment of workers, differences in the levels of pay and conditions of work between developing and developed countries should not be made the pretext for protectionism; access to markets should not be conditional on the adoption of labour standards inappropriate to the level of development (5.14).

H. Structural Adjustment
1. Assistance to individuals and enterprises should not be given in forms that encourage the retention of resources in activities in developed countries that are more suited to developing countries (5.4).

2. Governments should formulate and implement positive adjustment policies and mechanisms of assistance which encourage the mobility of resources through retraining and relocation so as to minimise the transitional costs of shifting resources out of activities more suited to developing countries (5.4).

3. These policies and measures should be linked to and should support improved safeguard provisions (2.44, 7.8).

I. General
1. Markets in the centrally planned economies should be more open to trade with developing countries; this would have significant benefits in enlarging world demand for developing country exports (4.27).

2. The newly industrialising and other economically more advanced developing countries should join in the reduction of trade barriers as a contribution to the expansion of markets, especially for the products of other developing countries (4.28).

Appendix 1
Part IV of GATT
Trade and Development

Article XXXVI
Principles and Objectives

1. The contracting parties,

(a) recalling that the basic objectives of this Agreement include the raising of standards of living and the progressive development of the economies of all contracting parties, and considering that the attainment of these objectives is particularly urgent for less-developed contracting parties;

(b) considering that export earnings of the less-developed contracting parties can play a vital part in their economic development and that the extent of this contribution depends on the prices paid by the less-developed contracting parties for essential imports, the volume of their exports, and the prices received for these exports;

(c) noting, that there is a wide gap between standards of living in less-developed countries and in other countries;

(d) recognizing that individual and joint action is essential to further the development of the economies of less-developed contracting parties and to bring about a rapid advance in the standards of living in these countries;

(e) recognizing that international trade as a means of achieving economic and social advancement should be governed by such rules and procedures — and measures in conformity with such rules and procedures — as are consistent with the objectives set forth in this Article;

(f) noting that the CONTRACTING PARTIES may enable less-developed contracting parties to use special measures to promote their trade and development;

agree as follows.

2. There is need for a rapid and sustained expansion of the export earnings of the less-developed contracting parties.

141

3. There is need for positive efforts designed to ensure that less-developed contracting parties secure a share in the growth in international trade commensurate with the needs of their economic development.

4. Given the continued dependence of many less-developed contracting parties on the exportation of a limited range of primary products, there is need to provide in the largest possible measure more favourable and acceptable conditions of access to world markets for these products, and wherever appropriate to devise measures designed to stabilize and improve conditions of world markets in these products, including in particular measures designed to attain stable, equitable and remunerative prices, thus permitting an expansion of world trade and demand and a dynamic and steady growth of the real export earnings of these countries so as to provide them with expanding resources for their economic development.

5. The rapid expansion of the economies of the less-developed contracting parties will be facilitated by a diversification of the structure of their economies and the avoidance of an excessive dependence on the export of primary products. There is, therefore, need for increased access in the largest possible measure to markets under favourable conditions for processed and manufactured products currently or potentially of particular export interest to less-developed contracting parties.

6. Because of the chronic deficiency in the export proceeds and other foreign exchange earnings of less-developed contracting parties, there are important inter-relationships between trade and financial assistance to development. There is, therefore, need for close and continuing collaboration between the CONTRACTING PARTIES and the international lending agencies so that they can contribute most effectively to alleviating the burdens these less-developed contracting parties assume in the interest of their economic development.

7. There is need for appropriate collaboration between the CONTRACTING PARTIES, other intergovernmental bodies and the organs and agencies of the United Nations system, whose activities relate to the trade and economic development of less-developed countries.

8. The developed contracting parties do not expect reciprocity for commitments made by them in trade negotiations to reduce or remove tariffs and other barriers to the trade of less-developed contracting parties.

9. The adoption of measures to give effect to these principles and objectives shall be a matter of conscious and purposeful effort on the part of the contracting parties both individually and jointly.

Article XXXVII

Commitments

1.   The developed contracting parties shall to the fullest extent possible —
that is, except when compelling reasons, which may include legal reasons,
make it impossible — give effect to the following provisions:

(a)   accord high priority to the reduction and elimination of barriers to
products currently or potentially of particular export interest to less-
developed contracting parties, including customs duties and other
restrictions which differentiate unreasonably between such products
in their primary and in their processed forms;

(b)   refrain from introducing, or increasing the incidence of, customs
duties or non-tariff import barriers on products currently or
potentially of particular export interest to less-developed contracting
parties; and

(c)   (i) refrain from imposing new fiscal measures, and

(ii) in any adjustments of fiscal policy accord high priority to the
reduction and elimination of fiscal measures,

which would hamper, or which hamper, significantly the growth of
consumption of primary products, in raw or processed form, wholly
or mainly produced in the territories of less-developed contracting
parties, and which are applied specifically to those products.

2.   *(a)*   Whenever it is considered that effect is not being given to any of
the provisions of sub-paragraph *(a)*, *(b)* or *(c)* of paragraph 1, the matter
shall be reported to the CONTRACTING PARTIES either by the contracting
party not so giving effect to the relevant provisions or by any other
interested contracting party.

(b)   (i) The CONTRACTING PARTIES shall, if requested so to do by any
interested contracting party, and without prejudice to any
bilateral consultations that may be undertaken, consult with the
contracting party concerned and all interested contracting
parties with respect to the matter with a view to reaching
solutions satisfactory to all contracting parties concerned in
order to further the objectives set forth in Article XXXVI. In the
course of these consultations, the reasons given in cases where
effect was not being given to the provisions of sub-paragraph *(a)*,
(b) or *(c)* of paragraph 1 shall be examined.

(ii) As the implementation of the provisions of sub-paragraph
(a), *(b)* or *(c)* of paragaph 1 by individual contracting parties may
in some cases be more readily achieved where action is taken
jointly with other developed contracting parties, such consultation might, where appropriate, be directed towards this end.

(iii) The consultations by the CONTRACTING PARTIES might also, in appropriate cases, be directed towards agreement on joint action designed to further the objectives of this Agreement as envisaged in paragraph 1 of Article XXV.

3.   The developed contracting parties shall:

(a)   make every effort, in cases where a government directly or indirectly determines the resale price of products wholly or mainly produced in the territories of less-developed contracting parties, to maintain trade margins at equitable levels;

(b)   give active consideration to the adoption of other measures designed to provide greater scope for the development of imports from less-developed contracting parties and collaborate in appropriate international action to this end;

(c)   have special regard to the trade interests of less-developed contracting parties when considering the application of other measures permitted under this Agreement to meet particular problems and explore all possibilities of constructive remedies before applying such measures where they would affect essential interests of those contracting parties.

4.   Less-developed contracting parties agree to take appropriate action in implementation of the provisions of Part IV for the benefit of the trade of other less-developed contracting parties, in so far as such action is consistent with their individual present and future development, financial and trade needs taking into account past trade developments as well as the trade interests of less-developed contracting parties as a whole.

5.   In the implementation of the commitments set forth in paragraphs 1 to 4 each contracting party shall afford to any other interested contracting party or contracting parties full and prompt opportunity for consultations under the normal procedures of this Agreement with respect to any matter or difficulty which may arise.

Article XXXVIII

Joint Action

1.   The contracting parties shall collaborate jointly, within the framework of this Agreement and elsewhere, as appropriate, to further the objectives set forth in Article XXXVI.

2.   In particular, the CONTRACTING PARTIES shall:

(a)   where appropriate, take action, including action through international arrangements, to provide improved and acceptable condi-

tions of access to world markets for primary products of particular interest to less-developed contracting parties and to devise measures designed to stabilize and improve conditions of world markets in these products including measures designed to attain stable, equitable and remunerative prices for exports of such products;

(b) seek appropriate collaboration in matters of trade and development policy with the United Nations and its organs and agencies, including any institutions that may be created on the basis of recommendations by the United Nations Conference on Trade and Development;

(c) collaborate in analysing the development plans and policies of individual less-developed contracting parties and in examining trade and aid relationships with a view to devising concrete measures to promote the development of export potential and to facilitate access to export markets for the products of the industries thus developed and, in this connexion, seek appropriate collaboration with governments and international organizations, and in particular with organizations having competence in relation to financial assistance for economic development, in systematic studies of trade and aid relationships in individual less-developed contracting parties aimed at obtaining a clear analysis of export potential, market prospects and any further action that may be required;

(d) keep under continuous review the development of world trade with special reference to the rate of growth of the trade of less-developed contracting parties and make such recommendations to contracting parties as may, in the circumstances, be deemed appropriate;

(e) collaborate in seeking feasible methods to expand trade for the purpose of economic development, through international harmonization and adjustment of national policies and regulations, through technical and commercial standards affecting production, transportation and marketing, and through export promotion by the establishment of facilities for the increased flow of trade information and the development of market research; and

(f) establish such institutional arrangements as may be necessary to further the objectives set forth in Article XXXVI and to give effect to the provisions of this Part.

Source: GATT, *Basic Instruments and Selected Documents*, Vol. IV, March 1969.

Appendix 2

GATT Safeguards

Article XIX

Emergency Action on Imports of Particular Products

1.   (a)   If, as a result of unforeseen developments and of the effect of the obligations incurred by a contracting party under this Agreement, including tariff concessions, any product is being imported into the territory of that contracting party in such increased quantities and under such conditions as to cause or threaten serious injury to domestic producers in that territory of like or directly competitive products, the contracting party shall be free, in respect of such product, and to the extent and for such time as may be necessary to prevent or remedy such injury, to suspend the obligation in whole or in part or to withdraw or modify the concession.

  (b)   If any product, which is the subject of a concession with respect to a preference, is being imported into the territory of a contracting party in the circumstances set forth in sub-paragraph (a) of this paragraph, so as to cause or threaten serious injury to domestic producers of like or directly competitive products in the territory of a contracting party which receives or received such preference, the importing contracting party shall be free, if that other contracting party so requests, to suspend the relevant obligation in whole or in part or to withdraw or modify the concession in respect of the product, to the extent and for such time as may be necessary to prevent or remedy such injury.

2.   Before any contracting party shall take action pursuant to the provisions of paragraph 1 of this Article, it shall give notice in writing to the CONTRACTING PARTIES as far in advance as may be practicable and shall afford the CONTRACTING PARTIES and those contracting parties having a substantial interest as exporters of the product concerned an opportunity to consult with it in respect of the proposed action. When such notice is given in relation to a concession with respect to a preference, the notice shall name the contracting party which has requested the action. In critical circumstances, where delay would cause damage which it would be difficult to repair, action under paragraph 1 of this Article may be taken provisionally without prior consultation, on the condition that consultation shall be effected immediately after taking such action.

3. *(a)* If agreement among the interested contracting parties with respect to the action is not reached, the contracting party which proposes to take or continue the action shall, nevertheless, be free to do so, and if such action is taken or continued, the affected contracting parties shall then be free, not later than ninety days after such action is taken, to suspend, upon the expiration of thirty days from the day on which written notice of such suspension is received by the CONTRACTING PARTIES, the application to the trade of the contracting party taking such action, or, in the case envisaged in paragraph 1 *(b)* of this Article, to the trade of the contracting party requesting such action, of such substantially equivalent concessions or other obligations under this Agreement the suspension of which the CONTRACTING PARTIES do not disapprove.

(b) Notwithstanding the provisions of sub-paragraph *(a)* of this paragraph, where action is taken under paragraph 2 of this Article without prior consultation and causes or threatens serious injury in the territory of a contracting party to the domestic producers of products affected by the action, that contracting party shall, where delay would cause damage difficult to repair, be free to suspend, upon the taking of the action and throughout the period of consultation, such concessions or other obligations as may be necessary to prevent or remedy the injury.

Source: GATT, *Basic Instruments and Selected Documents*, Vol. IV, March 1969.

Appendix 3

A Note on Country Groupings

Many of the country groupings used in this Report represent usage by different international agencies. Where a grouping has a precise definition it is provided below:

1. *OPEC*: Organization of Petroleum Exporting Countries. The members of OPEC are: Algeria, Ecuador, Gabon, Indonesia, Iran, Iraq, Kuwait, Libya, Nigeria, Qatar, Saudi Arabia, United Arab Emirates and Venezuela.

IMF and IBRD Definitions

2. *Oil-Exporting Countries*: Those countries from each of which average oil exports (net of any crude oil imports) in 1978-80 amounted to at least two-thirds of the value of total exports, and were at least 100 million barrels a year. These are Algeria, Indonesia, Iran, Iraq, Kuwait, Libya, Nigeria, Oman, Qatar, Saudi Arabia, United Arab Emirates and Venezuela.

3. *Non-Oil Developing Countries*: All developing countries other than those listed at 2 above.

4. *Net Oil Exporters*: Those developing countries that export more oil than they import but which are outside the group defined at 2 above. They are Bahrain, Bolivia, Congo, Ecuador, Egypt, Gabon, Malaysia, Mexico, Peru, Syria, Trinidad & Tobago and Tunisia.

5. *Net Oil Importers*: All developing countries except those listed in 2 and 4 above.

6. *Major Exporters of Manufactures*: All middle-income (see 10 below) net oil importers having relatively large exports of manufactures. The group includes Argentina, Brazil, Greece, Hong Kong, Israel, Rep. of Korea, Portugal, Singapore, South Africa and Yugoslavia. This group overlaps to a large extent with the "newly industrialising countries" (17 below).

7. *Other Net Oil Importers* (sometimes also referred to as *Middle-Income Primary Producing Countries*): All middle-income countries (as defined at 10 below) that export mainly primary commodities. Included in this group are all countries defined at 3 that are not included in 4, 6 or 9.

8. *Low-Income Developing Countries*: All countries whose 1979 per capita income was no more than $370. Comprises Burma, China, Guinea-Bissau, India, Indonesia, Kampuchea, Kenya, Madagascar, Mauritania, Pakistan, Sri Lanka, Vietnam, Zaire and all least developed countries (see 15 below) except Botswana, Djibouti, Equatorial Guinea, Sao Tome & Principe, Western Samoa, Yemen and Yemen Democratic Republic.

9. *Low-Income Oil Importers*: All low-income developing countries, except Indonesia.

10. *Middle-Income Developing Countries*: Those developing countries with 1979 per capita income above $370. Includes Spain which the IMF does not consider to be a developing country.

UN and UNCTAD Definitions

11. *Major Oil Exporting Countries*: Those developing countries for which petroleum and petroleum products accounted for more than half of their total exports in 1974. These are the countries named in 2 above, together with Angola, Bahrain, Brunei, Congo, Ecuador, Gabon, and Trinidad & Tobago. This is a larger category than group 2 above.

12. *Non-Oil Exporting Developing Countries*: All developing countries other than the major oil exporting developing countries as defined at 11 above. This is a smaller category than that defined at 3 above. Excludes Greece, Israel, Portugal, South Africa, Spain, Turkey, Romania and China which are not considered as developing countries by UNCTAD.

13. *Oil-Importing Developing Countries*: Non-oil exporting developing countries as defined at 12 above, other than Bolivia, Egypt, Malaysia, Mexico, Peru, Syria, Tunisia and Zaire.

14. *Fast-Growing Exporters of Manufactures*: Those developing countries with a per capita income greater than $1,000 in 1977 having exports of manufactures averaging more than 20 per cent of total exports in 1970-77 and growing in volume at an average annual rate of more than 8 per cent. The countries included in this group are Argentina, Brazil, Rep. of Korea, Singapore, Uruguay and Yugoslavia, and certain territories such as Hong Kong. This grouping overlaps to a considerable extent with 6 above and 17 below.

15. *Least Developed Countries*: Three basic criteria for this category were adopted in the mid-1960s: per capita GDP of $100 or less, a share of manufacturing of 10 per cent or less of GDP, and a population with 20 per cent or less of literate persons aged 15 years or more. The following 36 countries are at present recognised as such: Afghanistan, Bangladesh, Benin, Bhutan, Botswana, Burundi, Cape Verde, Central African Republic, Chad, Comoros, Djibouti, Equatorial Guinea, Ethiopia, The Gambia, Guinea, Guinea-Bissau, Haiti, Laos, Lesotho, Malawi, Maldives, Mali, Nepal, Niger, Rwanda, Sao Tome & Principe, Sierra Leone, Somalia, Sudan, Tanzania, Togo, Uganda, Upper Volta, Western Samoa, Yemen and Yemen Democratic Republic.

GATT Definition

16. *Industrial Countries*: These are defined to include the United States, Canada, Japan, the member countries of the EEC and EFTA, Gibraltar, Malta, Spain, Turkey and Yugoslavia. Excluded from this listing are Australia, New Zealand, South Africa, the countries of the Eastern Trading Area (viz. Albania, Bulgaria, Czechoslovakia, German Democratic Republic, Hungary, Poland, Romania, USSR, China, Mongolia, North Korea and Vietnam) as well as all developing countries.

OECD Definition

17. *Newly Industrialising Countries*: The so-called NICs are not usually referred to with a highly specific connotation, but by way of example the following countries were included for statistical purposes in the OECD study on "The Impact of the Newly Industrialising Countries" (1979) — Brazil, Greece, Hong Kong, Rep. of Korea, Mexico, Portugal, Singapore, Spain, Taiwan and Yugoslavia.

Appendix 4

Members of the Group of Experts

Sir Alec Cairncross (Chairman)	Chancellor, University of Glasgow; formerly Head of the U.K. Government Economic Service.
Prof. Mohamed Ariff	Professor of Analytical Economics and Dean, Faculty of Economics and Administration, University of Malaya.
Prof. Gerald K. Helleiner	Professor of Economics, University of Toronto; Vice-Chairman, North-South Institute, Ottawa.
Mr. Satya Nandan, CBE	Secretary for Foreign Affairs, Fiji; formerly Ambassador to Belgium and the European Communities.
Mr. Philip Ndegwa	Chairman, Kenya Commercial Bank Ltd.; formerly Economic Adviser to the President of Kenya.
Dr. Eric M. Ojala	Director, Centre for Agricultural Policy Studies, Massey University, New Zealand; formerly Assistant Director-General, FAO.
Mr. Frank B. Rampersad	President, National Institute for Higher Education, Research, Science and Technology, Trinidad & Tobago; Chairman, Trinidad & Tobago (BWIA International) Airways Corporation; formerly Director, Economic Affairs Division, Commonwealth Secretariat.
H.E. Mr. E. Olu Sanu	High Commissioner of Nigeria to Australia; formerly Ambassador to Belgium and the European Communities.
Dr. Manmohan Singh	Member Secretary, Planning Commission, Government of India; formerly Secretary to the Government of India in the Ministry of Finance.

151

Prof. Richard H. Snape	Professor of Economics, Monash University, Victoria, Australia; Member, Treasurer's Economic Panel, Australia.
Dr. Augustine Tan, M.P.	Member of Parliament and Associate Professor of Economics, National University of Singapore; formerly Political Secretary to Prime Minister, Singapore.
Secretariat	(Economic Affairs Division)
Dr. B. Persaud	Director (Secretary of Expert Group)
Mr. Q.S. Siddiqi	Assistant Director
Mr. D.R. Shipp	Assistant Director
Mr. I.R. Thomas	Chief Economics Officer
Mr. M.B. Rodgers	Chief Economics Officer